Praise for the Book

I have had the privilege of reading all of Sumita Banerjea's recent articles. Being a psychologist by training and practice, I am struck by how she uses her own life experiences—and empathetic observations of other people's lives—to bring out concepts to guide people in living more meaningfully and effectively.

Her articles are not pedantic or 'preachy'. She covers many aspects of our everyday living and gives us new insights or re-energises those we had 'forgotten'. Sumita helps us to unravel the dilemmas we face in our living today and 'simplify' the complexities of managing our relationships—including with ourselves.

—**Zahid Hoosein Gangjee**

Psychologist. Chief Executive, Zahid Gangjee & Associates, Organization and H.R. Consultancy, Kolkata. Honorary Fellow, Coaching Foundation of India

I have known Mrs Sumita Banerjea for a decade now and it is a pleasure writing a few words about her. As a counsellor she is honest and dedicated and works with utmost patience which makes the other person feel relaxed and comfortable during professional interactions.

Her writing is similarly a mirror of herself and her personality. She speaks on topics of extreme relevance in today's world where we often forget our priorities and things that matter the most. Her language is lucid and easy to understand and resonates easily with the reader. I wish her all success in her future endeavours.

—**Dr Sanjay Garg**

Psychiatrist. Head of the Department, Fortis Hospital, Anandapur, Kolkata

The articles are so beautifully written. Insightful, concise, easy to comprehend and each piece has something different to offer.

—**Mansi Poddar**
Psychotherapist and Founder,
Heal. Grow. Thrive Foundation

SCRIPT YOUR LIFE YOUR WAY

SUMITA BANERJEA

Readomania

Readomania
An imprint of Kurious Kind Media Private Limited
readomania.com
Email: contact@readomania.com
Facebook: facebook.com/iamreadomania
Twitter: twitter.com/iamreadomania
Instagram: iamreadomania

First Published in 2024 by Readomania

Edited by Indrani Ganguly (Managing Editor, Readomania)

ISBN: 978-93-91800-78-9

Typeset in Palatino Linotype by Shine Graphics
Printed in Delhi

Contents

Foreword

I feel honoured and privileged to be writing this foreword for Sumita Banerjea's book *Script Your Life Your Way.*

I have personally known Sumita for over a decade now. We first met at a workshop I was conducting and where she was participating. I experienced Sumita as a warm and intelligent person. Her sharpness in integrating the content was clearly evident through her questions and reflections.

We kept in touch with each other even though I moved cities. Sharing the same profession allowed us to discuss and share experiences and learn from each other.

I co-founded ***InfinumGrowth,*** an online magazine in 2017, focused on articles about personal growth and development, written by professionals from different sectors in the field of human psychology and behaviour and professional management.

We invited Sumita Banerjea to contribute articles for this magazine. Since 2020, Sumita has been one of our most popular and consistent authors.

She has this unique qualification of being a Historian, an Educator and a Counsellor, which makes her an expansive writer. Her professional experiences in these different fields bring the richness to her writings.

Sumita, despite being a professional in the field of Psychology, has kept her writing simple and crisp, attracting a large number of people to read them and relate with the ideas. Her anecdotes, stories, examples; all make for an interesting reading.

In this book, her focus has been on two aspects—one, looking within and understanding our personality at a deeper level; and second, looking around us and understanding our relationships.

Each of her articles is written with practical experiences shared or examples quoted, to illustrate issues which all of us face in life at one point or the other.

This makes it easy for anyone to grasp the human psychology and behaviour messages she provides, enabling us to incorporate these takeaways into our own lives.

I wish all her readers a great time reading the articles in this book, introspecting and bringing about positive change in their lives.

My best wishes to Sumita Banerjea to keep up the great work!

Ragini Rao

Teaching & Supervising Transactional Analyst (TSTA);
Psychotherapist & Trainer. Co-Founder, InfinumGrowth

Author's Note

"What does 'honeywalk' mean, Mamma?" asked the curious Baby Bear.

"Oh it is the dream walk where your life is easy and you get what you want with very little effort," replied Mamma Bear.

"You mean I can get to find all the delicious honey without having to hunt for it?" squealed Baby Bear, excitedly.

"You could say that, dear," answered Mamma Bear, with an indulgent smile.

"That would be so...o...o much Fun!" Baby Bear could barely contain his eager anticipation of swimming in a pool of honey.

"But darling, how would you know it is fun if you got it all the time? It would be common and mundane," quizzed Mamma Bear.

Baby Bear looked questioningly at his mother. "What does mundane mean, Mamma?"

"Something that is ordinary, dull, commonplace and not very interesting," she replied.

"Finding honey is very interesting, especially the way you do it, searching in the holes in trees. It is like a treasure hunt. And when you find it we have such a feast! It is not at all dull, Mamma."

"Exactly, dear. It is like a treasure hunt. And when we find the treasure it is thrilling to achieve something, isn't it? We value the honey even more and it tastes even more delicious!"

Life is a HAPPENING place. Like a steep hill drive—climbing up, going down and climbing up again with occasional hair-pin bends. Physical and mental fitness makes the journey easier, giving us the bandwidth to enjoy the view as we go along.

There are treasures and challenges we encounter—within and outside of us. The idea is to find the treasures, the joys and sparks in life, the honey—but we are often stuck in the dilemmas of our own minds.

The purpose of this book is to help us manage these hurdles, challenge our own unhelpful beliefs, discover our own strengths and lead a more productive and meaningful life, savouring the taste of the honey.

The chapters of this book have anecdotes drawn from my life experience. The characters have been fictionalized but the incidents reflect what many of us have either personally experienced or seen happening in the lives of those around us. The suggestions given to deal with issues that come up are helpful, doable and possible to implement.

To get the full benefit from the book, I would urge you to read the chapters carefully, notice if you see a bit of yourself in any of them and if you wish, answer the questions given at the end to hopefully gain some clarity.

These chapters have been previously published on an online platform https://www.infinumgrowth.com.

Sumita Banerjea

Part I
Journey Within

1

Courage

Essential for Living a Full and Empowered Life

A contentious post on a WhatsApp group led to an uproar. Many were extremely unhappy. After a couple of days, there was an apology posted by the erring member. What amazed me was what followed.

Those same agitated voices responded individually, appreciating the apology as a courageous act. It got me pondering about courage. A view attributed to psychologist Martin Seligman is that being courageous maximises one's chance to grow and develop throughout life.

What is courage?

I remember reading that courage is a psychological muscle! An unusual take but one that made sense. It is to do with the mind and how we decide to handle situations, such as adversity, intimidation, danger, uncertainty, risks, suffering, grief, fear, letting go of habits and addictions, admitting a wrong, persevering in the face of failure, standing firm with a moral conviction and so on.

The dictionary meaning is, "the ability to do something that frightens one" and "strength in the face of pain or grief". There is a saying that courage and fear are brothers. Nelson Mandela said, *"I learned that courage was not the absence of fear, but the triumph over it."*

Even if it is a physical act of courage, like skydiving, bungee jumping, facing a strong opponent in a boxing ring, going into battle or physically fighting off an attacker, the mind has to say "Ready, Get Set, Go". It requires courage.

Everyday Acts of Courage

The truth is that most of us, in our various walks of life, do little acts of courage in our regular routine; without ever giving it a label or even being aware of it.

Crossing a busy street, driving on a highway with monstrous vehicles coming from the other side, sometimes pushing us to the edge of the road; doctors performing risky and complicated surgeries; lifting a pot of boiling liquid or food while cooking; labourers working at high rises—are all acts where we show courage without even realising.

Other situations like batsmen facing fast balls; patients facing the diagnosis of a fatal disease; a person saying sorry to someone; breaking up a relationship, taking an unpleasant but necessary decision; are all acts of courage which become a way of life.

It could be a physical act, taking an ethical stand or accepting a personal shortcoming, admitting it and doing something about it. We may have doubts, fears or apprehensions deep in our sinews, but we do what we need to, regardless.

We become aware of the act as one of courage, when someone else points it out; or, when we need to deliberate over a matter or a feeling; and then take a decision or an action despite feeling scared.

It is a conscious choice, freely made; and is often a learnt skill, that we can develop with practise, taking small baby steps to start with.

How does one build courage?

We require different skills to handle a variety of challenges. These include the following:

1. Assertive Communication

Take, for example, the experience of being bullied at home or in a work place. We often cower in fear or resign ourselves to our fate. Instead of passive, passive aggressive or aggressive communication, using the different techniques of **assertive communication** can be very helpful. It requires training and then the courage to use it. We can make it a part of our arsenal with practise. It makes us feel better about ourselves, establishes boundaries and earns us respect.

2. Courage of Conviction

We need to have the courage of our convictions to take a stand. Especially when we have to hold our own in matters of ethics or morality, believing it is the right thing to do. Rabindranath Tagore's stirring Bengali song, '*Ekla Cholo Re*', is about walking alone, unafraid, even if no one else responds to our call.

An employee in a firm, who refused to sign the balance sheet because he would not compromise on his ethics, since he knew that the figures were not right, is a case in point. He displayed courage in standing by his beliefs and also being willing to face the consequences of his decision. Acts of courage can have repercussions and cause pain, but we go ahead with the act because not doing it would in all likelihood cause more distress and pain in the long run.

3. Listening

Courage is not just about speaking up or doing something. It is also about listening; even to a negative feedback, acknowledging that the other person is justified in his or her point of view. It is sometimes about not doing something and just holding back. For example, a parent not repeatedly checking up on a teenager who is out with his friends, despite being anxious.

4. Faith and Affirmations

Faith and affirmations help build courage. Instead of focusing on what can go wrong, we could list all the resources (within and outside of us) we have, to deal with unwelcome surprises and affirm what we can do to handle situations and make things better.

Visualising a pleasant and happy image and projecting it into the future as a goal, is a good way of motivating oneself. The firm resolve ignites a power within us that gets manifested as courage. This does not mean that we are naive and become petulant if things do not actualise exactly as we had hoped. Affirmations help in reducing negativity in our thoughts and give us strength to hold on to hope and convictions that whatever happens, we will handle it.

Also, is it realistically possible to have a completely pain free life? The fear of pain gives it enormous power over our minds. A lady was suffering because of arthritis but the fear of painful rehabilitation after a knee replacement surgery stole her mental strength and the ability to even bear the thought of the pain. She became a victim of her own thoughts and continued to suffer by catastrophising the pain she thought she would feel.

It has often been said that things happen in life, not necessarily happy events all the time, but the challenge is how we respond to them—do we manage them with equanimity and courage or do we buckle under them and suffer? The suffering is invariably in our minds and thoughts, which we can try and control. Our thoughts are generated by us—how we manoeuvre them is up to us. And over time it is this ability to deal with tough times and challenges that gives us the innate courage to handle life's tough terrains.

Mind calming techniques of meditation, mindfulness, yoga and pranayama all help build our capacity to handle difficult situations. They help in making us more relaxed, attentive and alert.

Reading true life tales of courage or talking to people who have overcome personal hurdles is encouraging. We realise we are not alone in our struggles. Talking to those we hold close and can share our troubles with also helps in building strength and courage. Simply discussing matters helps bring clarity in thoughts and shows us options available.

It takes courage to have faith in and place ourselves into somebody's hands, such as a doctor, a financial adviser, a swimming instructor... To get that courage we must allow ourselves to be vulnerable sometimes and build trust.

5. Permission to Accept and Recognise Fears

Once we give ourselves permission to accept our fear and recognise it as an impediment in our life, we can build the courage and take action to overcome it. It is useful to be aware of the excuses we create to avoid taking a tough decision.

One way to build courage is to try and do something a little challenging each week to build our risk taking capacity. A lady decided to overcome her fear of driving on a busy street (despite having a license) by first driving around in her quiet neighbourhood, then took the car out on Sundays when the traffic was much less, graduated to driving with someone by her side on weekdays and is now a confident driver.

List out your major fears, speak them out loud (this helps to minimise their unsaid and unvoiced magnitude), write how they are hampering your life and those around you; and then, think of how to resolve them sensibly.

After prioritising, work on them, one at a time. Sometimes they are interlinked. For example, we may have a fear of confrontation and the resultant tension. There could be a fear of losing our position at work and so we allow ourselves to be bullied and tell ourselves that it is our destiny and there is nothing we can do in the circumstances. These two fears are interlinked and handling one helps the other too.

Fear is also an emotion that is in our mind—of what CAN happen. We could try and take the wind out of its sails, by challenging it and doing a reality check. We also need to be aware of and emotionally prepared for the consequences of our action or inaction.

6. Fear—as a weakness

Fear can also make us weak. A woman found herself in the clutches of a soothsayer who fed on her fear and duped her of vast amounts; getting her to buy expensive stones and doing *kriyas* (rituals) costing thousands, to ward off evil in her life.

With help from people she was close to, she picked up the courage to break out of his tentacles and the 'comfort' he provided; and could take her own decisions. The independence she experienced was a huge reward. But to get there, she first had to accept and understand her quandary and then ask for help.

7. Fear—as a protection

Of course one must also remember that some fears are protective for us. Disregarding all fears and showing unnecessary bravado, being foolhardy or impulsive, just to make a point or sometimes doing things on a dare, could result in physical or mental harm. We need to be balanced.

Fear of things that can bring us physical harm (example: not exposing ourselves to unnecessary risks in a Covid infested world) and staying off situations and people who threaten our mental peace, not being reckless and joining a herd act simply to win acceptance, are things we need to keep in mind.

Doing this analysis/evaluation gives us the space to rationally decide what we need to work on and what we can allow to remain, in our own interest.

8. Courage grows when we look beyond ourselves

Suchitra faced a hard time with her parents-in-law. Brought up with beliefs like one should never answer back elders, she lost her voice when she needed to say anything to them when she felt wronged. She had a two-year-old child and a nanny to help her. The nanny and she were close and in her she found a companion. The in-laws resented the fact that the nanny was not in their control and tried to find faults with her on a regular basis. Suchitra noticed this and the irritation in her built up—till one day when she succeeded in doing what she had been unable to do for herself. She faced them head on and spoke her mind clearly and firmly on behalf of the nanny. She found the courage to look beyond her own fears to stand up for another human being who she felt was being ill treated. Of course, the recipients of her outrage were shocked into silence but more importantly she had found her voice.

Here is another relevant story. *A young boy from an affluent family took to drugs. The habit consumed his life—his health, relationships, educational pursuit and future prospects. He recalls. "I would scrounge the public waste bins for food because my family had given up on me." What made him change? "I met a friend from a rehab centre I had gone to and found that he had discovered a purpose in his life by joining a centre for homeless people. He helped there and had given up the habit. I took courage and hope from him. Perhaps I could be useful to someone else too. I joined a rehab centre and worked very sincerely. Having gone through the darkest pits in life I could help from a place of understanding and hope. It required a lot of courage and discipline but here I am, running this centre for the past decade and helping others."*

Benefits of courage

1. An act of courage is often liberating for us

It frees us from mental tussles: "Should I or should I not? What if I am ostracised? Will people laugh at me? The risk may not be worth it. This is too difficult to do."

Responding from the space of fear is common, does not require much mental bandwidth and is usually a short-term stress reliever. Over the long haul it is more prudent to work with the fear that is driving the response.

2. Courage is empowering

Doing something tough, despite being scared, builds self confidence and self esteem. We feel good about ourselves.

Acknowledging and giving up an addiction, doing things despite physical or mental challenges (remember Sudha Chandran who continued to dance, despite amputation and a prosthetic Jaipur foot?), standing up for oneself, learning the use of devices that appeared overwhelming, trying to materialise a dream, public speaking—are all acts of courage, that are empowering.

As a stronger, self confident person, one can live a fuller life, without being debilitated by fears. We can also be of help to others, giving them support in building courage.

> *"Courage doesn't always roar. Sometimes courage is the little voice at the end of the day that says I'll try again tomorrow."*
>
> **—Mary Anne Radmacher**

Introspection

1. What is the most courageous act that you have done?
2. Can you recall the feeling you experienced before and after doing the act? Do you like to think of yourself as a courageous person?
3. Of the skills mentioned in the article for being courageous, which one do you find most challenging?
4. How could you enhance the skill? What is your challenge in being courageous?
5. Think of the special qualities in a person you know or have heard about who displays courage.

2

Limiting Beliefs within Us

Becoming Aware and Making Changes

"If you accept a limiting belief, then it will become a truth for you."

—Louise Hay

The term Limiting Beliefs means exactly what the literal meaning is—any belief that is limiting for us. There are limiting beliefs that act as a check on us, stopping us from indulging in illegal, anti-social, unethical or dangerous acts. These are helpful limiting beliefs that keep us safe. But there are many limiting beliefs that are unhelpful; stopping us from leading a satisfactory life.

Unhelpful limiting beliefs

In this chapter, we will focus on the unfavourable limiting beliefs—that limit us in multiple ways; in our perspectives, as a barrier in our personal growth, in the way we interact with people; and therefore in our overall happiness in life.

These are limiting beliefs that put us into a prison of our own making. Most often we are oblivious to the walls and barricades since we are oblivious to the fact that we are in a prison.

Certain thought and behavioural patterns become dead habits, based on our constricting beliefs and **we are reduced to mere bodies inhabiting those habits**, without the ability to think, question or analyse them.

More often than not, we are so controlled by our limiting beliefs that we act according to them to prove them right; like a self fulfilling prophecy. And then we are further convinced that we are right/justified in our beliefs.

Shoulds and *Should nots* in one's belief system

Many of these beliefs are imbibed as 'should' and 'should not' from childhood and get ingrained into us without our being aware. At times we get stuck in the quagmire of superstitions because of this. Sometimes when someone else points them out and if we are open to introspection we realise how cramping they can be.

"Today is Wednesday. I cannot cut my nails," said Ankit.

"Why?" asked Anita.

"It is the day of the week I was born and one should not cut one's nails on that day."

This was his firm 'should not' belief. It took a fair amount of effort from Anita to help him challenge and question this, before he accepted it as simply an unfounded belief.

Superstitions can become so powerful that if, by chance, anything were to go wrong after he cut his nails on a Wednesday, he would put it down to going against his belief; and he would probably pass this belief down to the next generation.

Inbuilt fears in our beliefs

For years, Kanika believed that she would collapse if she had to address a gathering. So deep seated was this conviction that any mention of talking to a large audience would result in a serious panic attack.

This belief robbed her of chances of a promotion at work, of opportunities to take on new challenges and of her self confidence. Then, one day, when both her line seniors at work were away, there was an emergency that required her to address a large gathering of her team and clients.

She broke into a cold sweat. Her breathing became shallow and her mouth was parched. But she had no way out. The job had to be done. Mustering up her shredded courage she wrote down what needed to be conveyed. She kept a glass of water next to her; told herself that the worst that could happen was that she would be hauled up for doing her job unsatisfactorily and got herself to the podium on trembling legs.

Getting off to a shaky start she managed to read her speech aloud; and then, gradually, felt calmer with some deep breathing and sips of water. Her announcement evoked queries from the audience. She was confident about her content and slowly started answering the questions. The session went on for over an hour.

It was an hour that proved to be a milestone in her life.

Without this emergency happening that pushed her to the tipping point, she could very easily have lived her life believing that she was incapable of addressing an audience.

What was required for a more permanent resolution was understanding where the fear or anxiety of facing an audience/ fear of failure/judgement came from and whether it got manifested in other areas too and dealing with that, instead of converting it into a limiting belief about herself.

Examples of Limiting Beliefs—regarding ourselves and the world at large

1. Beliefs that we have regarding ourselves, as inferior or superior to others

"I'm not good enough to handle this responsibility."

"I am not attractive or lovable and will never find a partner."

"I must not give my opinion in a group because I always end up saying something stupid."

"They will not find anyone as suited as me to handle this and they can't seem to see that."

"It is a waste of time spending time with them because their intellect does not match mine."

2. Belief that I know what the person is actually saying, by pre-deciding without even listening

This could make us over suspicious, critical and unable to trust or delegate. It may come from the belief that people are out to get us.

"I don't trust people because they don't mean what they say—there is an underlying agenda."

3. Belief based on negative expectations

Starting out with a negative thought when considering any project is bound to have an impact on how much effort and commitment we are willing to invest in it.

"Given my luck, I am sure there will be a last minute hiccup and the project will be given to someone else."

4. Belief based on fear

"I don't want to allow myself to feel extremely happy because something sad invariably happens soon after."

5. Beliefs that limit one's spontaneity

"I am keen on trying out some adventure sports but it is far too late now and people will laugh at me."

How do limiting beliefs limit us?

- They could hinder us from being open to constructive feedback, making our boundaries of expansion and growth shrink
- They could block us from being open to new ideas or other options, hence fresh opportunities are lost
- They could impact our relationships
- They often outlive their validity but continue to be held
- Stop us from thinking out of the box
- For leaders, limiting beliefs can limit us from accepting and embracing new ideas and innovations
- Stop us even before we get started in trying something different or new because of a fear of some repercussion and this takes away our agency.

How do we get out of this loop?

The idea is to be fair to oneself and give permissions to embrace life with all its avenues for growth and happiness. Make choices in areas that are in our control and do what we can.

As Brendon Burchard said, ***"I'm not interested in your limiting belief, I'm interested in what makes you limitless."*** For starters, we must be open to questioning ourselves, be flexible to change, be humble about accepting another view if it seems more rational and convincing and be open to people who might point out the flaws in some of our beliefs. An objective view from a third person is often an eye opener, telling us where we can improve.

It is not that we become any *less* if we change or amend our views. Quite the contrary. Time moves, we grow, situations change and a belief that made sense at a certain point in time may not be applicable now.

Here are some ways to help oneself:

1. Be aware that a particular belief is unhelpful

The belief is limiting because amongst other things it might make us feel anxious and low, prevent us from mixing freely with friends, make us over critical and judgemental of others, make us think up excuses or complain that life is unfair, make us pressurise ourselves to excel and thus not enjoy the activity.

Repeatedly facing the same problem is a signal to stop and think about the cause; the beliefs that are driving this. For example, if the belief is that there is no point in discussing or verbalising something that is troubling me in a relationship because it will only lead to confrontation and no solution, then I will find myself repeatedly getting hurt. So I need to step back and see why I am getting hurt. Has **not** talking about it led to any resolution? Is there anything else that I could do or perhaps see how I can express myself calmly?

Is it my fear of confrontation that holds me back and could I learn helpful methods of communication to handle that?

If the belief is that the world MUST be nice to me then I am likely to be disappointed or if the belief is that I MUST be perfect in whatever I do then chances are that I will constantly be stressed out.

2. Reword an unhelpful belief

For example, "If I had the money I would live a much happier life" could be reworded to "I have enough resources to do so many little things that add a spark to each day". This way, instead of whining and thinking about all that I cannot do, I appreciate and enjoy all the little joys that I am living and experiencing each day.

"I am far too old to enrol for the course." Reword it to, "I have the life experience to get much more from the course now than I did ten years ago." Or "I know that I will enjoy the course since I am doing it because I really want to learn something new."

"I cannot get out of this long toxic relationship because I cannot hurt my parents/of what people will say." We keep avoiding taking a hard decision even though we are suffering. Reword this to, "I have tried long enough and now I need to get out of this relationship and lead a happier life. I could also take time out and stay by myself to see what life would be like. I have options open to me. I know my parents want me to be happy. I need to live *my* life and not be influenced by what people think."

It is an empowering thought that makes us feel more confident and sure of our course of action. We give ourselves the chance of beginning afresh and leading a richer and more meaningful, productive and peaceful life.

3. Get to the source of the limiting belief

Ask yourself what makes you hold on to it. Perhaps as a child you were told that you had no 'eye' for drawing, or your fingers were too small to learn to play the piano, or that it is a waste of time and money to hang out with friends or that it is a sign of being vain and conceited to pamper oneself and take care to look good…the list is endless.

Question it, look for evidence and check its authenticity. Sift the evidence from the assumptions.

4. Challenge the limiting belief by generating a counter belief

Repeat it to yourself and then practise it. 'Practice makes it perfect' is a saying we have all heard. It takes a long time to establish a belief, helpful or unhelpful. To alter it will take time too; and we need to be patient and consistent, knowing that we are working on it for the longer good.

5. Write down the limiting beliefs and the new counter beliefs

It helps to write the original limiting beliefs and the counter beliefs that challenge them. "I cannot handle confrontations." To challenge this we could write, "I can always learn the skill of assertive and effective communication." Putting them down on paper makes them more 'real' and visible. It is possible that a counter belief may not pan out as planned. We give it an honest try and then if it does not work try something else.

"I cannot learn singing because I have been told that I am tone deaf." To challenge this we could write, "I love music and it makes me so happy. I will learn singing for my own happiness. I don't need to become a public performer."

Working on our limiting beliefs is like becoming a 'self-detective'; finding the 'culprit' within us, getting help if needed to understand the problem and taking correctional measures, to lead a happier and more fulfilling life.

> *" Nothing binds you except your thoughts; nothing limits you except your fear; and nothing controls you except your beliefs." EVERYTHING is within you.*
>
> **– Marianne Williamson**

Introspection

1. Can you think of a belief that you carry about yourself that has stopped you from exploring new dimensions or limited you from utilising your full potential?
2. If you can isolate a limiting belief that you might have about yourself, think of a time when you challenged it or visualise how you might challenge it. What did it or will it make possible for you?
3. Think of the limiting beliefs you might be passing down unconsciously to the next generation or to those who might be looking up to you as their team leader or mentor. How could you help them grow to their full potential?

4. Make two columns on a piece of paper. On one side list the beliefs that have limited you and write how they might have controlled your growth and stopped you from spreading your wings. On the opposite write the things you could do if the belief was not there.

3

Memories are Lifelong Resources

Recently when we were to visit our son and his family, I asked him if there was anything in particular that we could take across for our four-year-old granddaughter. "Ma, don't get her things. She has enough. Think of what you can do along with her and get what you need for doing that."

I delved into a four-year-old me, thinking of what I enjoyed then and what came up was a world totally alien to the one today.

I did not have a TV, games on an iPad, gadgets of all kinds, but I had vivid memories of very happy times from my childhood. They revolved around people of whom I have specific memories.

Many memories stay with us through life

Each person had left a unique imprint and had his or her speciality—of telling wondrous stories, playing and creating exciting adventurous games, building little toy houses with bricks and cardboard and cooking the most delectable food items.

I also have good memories of people creating fascinating jewellery; moulding moist clay into all kinds of shapes and baking them; making wobbly paper boats and floating them in big puddles in the rain.

Of climbing the guava and mango trees to pluck the juiciest of fruits; bathing the pet dog; and of me getting thoroughly drenched when the dog gave a mighty wet shrug.

A child then and a child now is essentially the same even if the setting is different. I could try and create happy memories of activities done together that were customised to just the two of us—which no television cartoon or iPad game could hijack.

Building memories

That is exactly what I did; I told her animated stories and got her to make bookmarks with characters from those stories; played word games and encouraged her to tell me her wondrous stories of big stripy happy tigers that jumped down from the sky, to play with unicorns that needed parachutes to fly.

I then typed these onto my iPad and showed her. I made crepe-paper flowers with her and arranged them in empty juice bottles; and also baked peanut butter cookies which she shaped into little bunnies, carrots and flowers with cookie cutters.

In short, we hopefully created pleasant memories which will be filed away in her 'mind-book of childhood remembrances'.

Memories that will give her succour when, as an adult, she takes a quiet moment to revisit and reflect on the years gone by.

Visual memories and associated emotions

In fact, today when I look back at my life, decade by decade, what I see are a string of visual memories and feel the emotions associated with them. Visual memories are capricious and have a habit of changing form and time.

But the associated emotion, happy or not, can still give a tug. A familiar aroma from our past, associations with a song, feelings tied to places, perhaps a rocking chair... They are sources of comfort.

If not a source of comfort, they are a source of learning and acceptance; of the many different threads in the tapestry called life. Memories of trials and tribulations stay as red flags somewhere in our minds, acting as guides in later life.

Many of us struggle with some memories and have difficulty dealing with them, processing them and in some way healing them. They tend to make us feel stuck and hinder us from embracing and enjoying life in the present. There are choices open to us and each one must decide what to do.

Thus, memories become resources for us, that we can access and use in the calm or turbulent waters of life.

Importance of memories

Imagine a time when you lose all your memory from your phone. No tap of a button to read your messages, view your photo gallery or check your email. You feel a little lost, right? And disconnected too!

Now imagine waking up one morning and realising that your own memory has been wiped clean. You try desperately to remember your own name, the numbers or the letters of the alphabet, what you ate for dinner the night before...it is all lost to recall.

What would you feel? Utter helplessness; a sense of vacuum, where you are floating around in nothingness with no anchor. Right? It would be quite terrifying, actually.

1. Memories create our sense of identity

Our memory and what meaning we make of our stored experiences constitute who we are. I may have grown up spending a lot of fun-filled time outdoors and look for opportunities to do the same later.

On the other hand, a traumatic memory associated with exploring the outdoors will possibly make me very cautious of it later in life.

Our personal memories and how we have interpreted them, give us a sense of identity. It is our knowledge and our 'felt' emotions base that provide stability and continuity.

2. Our memory bank as a DNA

Every person's memory bank is almost like one's DNA; because no two persons' memory 'chip' will have exactly the same data.

There is a feeling of ownership that we feel. Each of us has unique memories and narratives depending on perspective and processing even if we go through the same experience.

3. Memories form a web

Memories get attached to other memories and form a web. Memory of an incident is often linked to a person, a place, a certain time of day or season; and we get access to a complete mosaic.

When we are feeling low, positive memories can help us appreciate the good things that have happened; and understand that there is a balance in life.

4. Memories as a feeling of social connect

They give us a feeling of social connectedness when we discuss and share memories.

Sharing memories of school or college days with friends, recalling incidents at family get-togethers with relatives, exchanging favourite songs of a particular era... we can keep adding to the list.

We 'lock' memories in pictures and videos and looking at them later helps in remembering those who may no longer be with us anymore.

5. Memories as a fountain of life

Poetically put, our cache of memories is our fountain of life, which we dip into to build the present and the future. Happy memories can be a balm in unhappy times. They can be a driving force for hopes, values, self image, sense of purpose and confidence.

A group of friends were sharing memories about their school teachers. One of them recalled an incident of when she was in Class 2. "We looked forward to the ice-cream vendor who was allowed into the school twice a week. I loved the cream sandwich—vanilla ice cream between two chocolate biscuits. My parents and brother had never tasted it and I wanted them to have it too. So one day when the ice-cream man came I bought one with the money my mother had given me and put it into my bag. In my excitement I forgot that the ice cream would melt which it did and leaked all over my things. My classmates made fun of me and called me stupid and some teachers too laughed at my mistake. But one teacher came up to me, put her hands on my shoulder and told the class, 'You all only saw the melted ice cream but could not see the love with which she was hoping to share it with her family. How many of you thought of sharing with your family when enjoying the treat?' I'll never forget that moment and how good I felt. I treasure the memory."

Equally important is if we notice an unhelpful pattern of behaviour in our memory bank, of how we respond to certain situations, we might wish to improve upon it and work towards changing it.

Sahil was agitated when an error in his presentation was pointed out by his boss, and he responded very immaturely. He was given a warning. He soon realised that his behaviour had been inappropriate and thought about the matter. It struck him that in the past too he had not taken criticism well even from others. His memory of his ill-mannered behaviour pattern in those situations helped him to work on himself in the future.

6. Memories as a knowledge base

There is also the pure academic aspect. What we learn as we grow becomes our knowledge base, our foundation stone to build upon and grow further.

If our interest in a subject is deep and we find it meaningful, chances are that we will remember it better and faster. The advantage is that it can be erased or worked upon, if later learnings disprove what we have learnt and remembered previously. So the content in this memory file can be updated.

What we need to be careful about

- Accept that memories are just that—meaning, that they are a blend of facts and figments of our imagination. And they are fluid. They change, fade and we might give them a fresh coat of paint which might be close to the original event, but not an exact replica. As neurologist Oliver Sacks explained, "We now know that memories are not fixed or frozen, like Proust's jars of preserves in a larder, but are transformed, disassembled, reassembled, and recategorized with every act of recollection."
- Rigidity in claiming that our recollection of something is the only authentic one, leads to unnecessary tension and disagreements. Each person remembers it from his or her experience of it; and that is fine.
- We cannot get so attached to memories that we simply live in the past and forget to get on with the present. Mindfulness is all about living and experiencing the present moment. In the next moment it becomes a memory. Change is said to be the only constant; and, the faster we accept this, the better it will be, for our mental health.
- We sometimes tend to glorify the memories of past events and give them attributes, which in all likelihood is not the complete picture. *"In our times, things were so much better. People were kinder, more honest. Today we only see selfishness all around..."* Sounds familiar?
- The reverse is also true. In our memory we may make past events appear to be much darker than they were; and end up putting ourselves in the victim position.

A memory is a thing of the past. We experienced something in a different time and place. It cannot be recreated in the present in the exact same way. Expecting to have the same experience and feel the same feelings, almost always leads to disappointment. Keep the two distinct.

We might have a childhood memory of really relishing a particular dish in a restaurant. We visit it years later based on that memory, and hope to have the same thrill. Years have passed by, we may have eaten similar dishes at other places, our preferences may have changed subconsciously, the taste buds and our minds may have got jaded with age and the ability to have a magical experience may have diminished.

Even our hunger pangs may be quite different from the time we tasted it first. Quite obviously, chances are that after having the meal we will say, *"Oh, the quality and taste is no longer the same as it used to be. It would have been better to just remember the taste as it was."*

How would we like to be remembered?

Finally, we come to the logical question at the end of this chapter. How would we like people to remember us?

Life is a continuous process of creating and generating memories. For us, it would be good to live today in a way that we minimise regret of its memory tomorrow.

To a large extent, what memories we create of ourselves, in the lives of those we interact with, is up to us.

And:

"Nothing is ever really lost to us as long as we remember it."

—LM Montgomery

Introspection

1. How powerful a role do memories have in your life?
2. Create a list of the happiest memories of every five years of your life. How do they make you feel now?
3. Memories are essentially feelings that we store in our mental hard drive. Would you agree?
4. Think of the people you have interacted with in the past twenty-four hours. What feelings have you left them with after your interaction with them? Would you like to change any of it? If yes then how would you do it?
5. How much do you allow unhappy memories to colour your present?

4

My Life Story

Creating My Own Script & Taking Charge of My Life

A popular exercise in a creative writing class is getting the students to write their own finale to a given story. One method is by changing the dialogue of the protagonist at crucial points.

I remember a student saying, *"Ma'am, I don't like the ending. It does not make me feel good."*

"So what can you do? Simply changing the last line will not do," I responded.

"I can change her thoughts," she replied promptly and continued, speaking aloud her take on the story. "She could make different choices. Instead of changing her school and running away because she was getting bullied, she could form a group of students who suffered like her or supported her. They could organise a protest petition. A group would be stronger and those bullying would think twice, before they did or said mean things."

The young student had thought through the process and realised that one can try to veer the story to a desired conclusion.

"Atta girl! That is the way to go. You are learning the ropes early in life," I thought to myself.

Life gives a framework for our personal story

Where and to whom we are born, opportunities provided to us, decisions taken for us when we are very young, societal and family influences are not matters we have control over. Call it destiny, circumstances or God's bigger plan for us. But **how we live our story**—fill in the details, the conversations, inner dialogues—**is up to us**.

The school, the bullies, the situations the girl was facing, were beyond her control. But she could choose to run away or face it intelligently and effectively and write **her** story accordingly.

How to script your own life story

Own it. It is never too late. When in a dilemma, certainly take help and advice but finally be your own author. Sometimes it is easier to delegate decisions to others but it is **you who** has to live it. Along the journey, certain decisions will need to be edited or altered and we need to be on top of the game, of how we take our life forward.

We need to be interactive and proactive with our own life. The truth is that we often become bystanders as our own life passes us by. We know that we cannot change the past. But we can change how we replay it in our internal dialogues and make new meanings from it.

As a result, we rewrite our responses to it in the present, in a way that it is more constructive and helpful to us. Even a small shift in perspective and retelling, can have a substantial impact on the future.

Shiuli held a deep grudge against her mother for what she felt was neglect during her upbringing. The feeling was toxic for her, affecting her in multiple ways. Finally, she sought help to process this feeling and as an adult understood the trauma that her mother suffered silently from the treatment meted out to her in her in-law's house. She had not been in a position to care for herself or her child. This new perspective changed her anger to compassion for her mother and helped in healing her and the relationship.

Live your thoughts and wishes. Japan has the concept of 'Ikigai'. It refers to anything, small or big, that gives a person a reason to live, a purpose in life, something to look forward to on waking up, even if it is having a steaming cup of tea. It is important that we find our Ikigai.

Take charge of the life story

Minal's school group posted a story of a classmate who had never been able to join her childhood mates for a weekend trip outside the city because of 'pressing' responsibilities at home. It seemed that she was indispensable.

And then she suddenly passed away. But her home, husband, children and in-laws managed fine after a short period of adjustment. This episode shook Minal and it resonated with her deeply.

A friend, who was a counsellor, suggested that Minal (in her late forties) write her life story and predict how she would want it to pan out. As she penned her life in words, decade by decade, she became increasingly conscious of the monotony of her existence and how conditioned she had become to it.

She could not remember when she had last done something different, challenged herself, felt really excited, enthused, and tinglingly alive. It was depressing to imagine the future following the same vein.

Even as a child she loved visiting butterfly and bird parks and had imagined becoming an ornithologist. Despite her abiding love for them, they had been relegated to a neglected corner of her life.

And the years were ticking away. No, she could not let her life get lost in a moribund state, with no cheer. She needed to take charge of her life story and she did.

Scripting the life story in the present tense

Life coaches suggest that you write the script in the present tense. Not as wishful thinking but as a live, palpable life that you are leading currently. It could be a personal achievement, a charitable act. Just word it as if it is actually happening.

"I am writing the first chapter of my book"; "I am ordering fifteen cardigans to give to the orphanage"; "Having lost five kilograms by doing intermittent fasting, I am feeling so much better"; "I've volunteered to help at the home for senior citizens thrice a week for two hours"; "I have fixed an appointment with the lawyer to understand the legal details of setting up my consultancy firm".

Doing this helps in putting urgency and actuality in the script. Believing in your story and having faith in yourself is important. So what follows is to write the script details, such that you take small steps to reach the goal.

Some important actions in the process are:

- Cheer yourself on as you achieve small targets. The destination will not appear impossible to reach.
- Share your ideas with those who wish you well, understand you and will support you. It is most natural to have questions and fears and having supportive voices always helps.
- Ask yourself, if your story was offered to you to write a book, would it interest you? In other words, does your own life interest you and does it seem interesting to you?
- Another question to ask is, "What would I not want to regret?" It helps in framing the episodes and filling in the details. An approximate timeframe for each episode is useful.

Given that life has a habit of throwing surprises, it is essential that we do not get obsessed and fixated with our own script. We need to have the mental flexibility to tweak it as and when necessary. Remember, if we are the authors, we own it.

How does scripting a life story help?

Not having a plan or a life story script does not mean that life goes astray and we lead a worthless existence. But we have limited time; and having a plan, pausing and reviewing how things are going, helps in self reflection, making changes to live our lives better and happier.

Scripting a Life Story helps in the following ways:

- It is an opportunity to make the gift of life more worthwhile. It gives us clarity of vision of where we are, where we aspire to be on different parameters and lets us chalk out a rough plan of how to get there. Each of us has different compartments in our lives—family and friends, our professional life and other responsibilities, our personal health, hobbies and aspirations and finally our role as a member of the society and what we can contribute there. It helps to take stock of how effectively we are functioning in the different compartments. There are pictures of the wellness wheel available on the internet that we can refer to and see for ourselves how we can apply it to our own life.

- Reviewing helps in getting back to base and understanding where the effort is sufficient or lacking. Also, life situations change and we can alter the script accordingly. We can flow with the river of life and be the coxswain of our boat.
- Having something written down gives a formal structure that we can refer to. It acts as an inspiration and a guide. Reading it aloud to ourselves regularly keeps us on track.
- Making a plan and detailing how we can actualise it, helps us to become aware of all our resources. Inside and around us.
- Affirming to ourselves that it will happen, helps in generating positive energy. We energise and re-charge ourselves.
- Finally, there is only so much that we can plan and prepare. There is always the unknown, unexpected and unanticipated element in life that might take us unawares.

And then we need to deal with it as best as we can; with the belief that "Good fortune is not forever and disappointments come and go. The choice is ours to continue, regardless."

—Anonymous

Introspection

1. On a scale of 0 to 10 if you feel that your happiness and contentment level is at say 5 and you want to be at 8, can you visualise how life would be different at 8? What could you do to make those things possible?
2. What are the areas in your life which you could exercise a hold over to make life more meaningful for yourself?
3. Go on—be the imaginative script writer owning your own life story, being engaged with it and tweaking it as you go along to make it more interesting and fulfilling.
4. How could you add diversity, depth and dreams to your life script? We can make our own lives more interesting for ourselves.

5

Self Discipline

Building the Will and Ability to Sustain it

Dear Discipline,

I have noticed that over the past few months you have been avoiding me. If you think that by hiding, you can lessen some burden on yourself, of getting me back on track, I have news for you!

There is a mole in your organisation that has wizened me up to your tricks; and to your new found friends, who wish to score a point over you; by making you relax and not do your job.

These 'non-friends' have cosied up to me, to ensure that our friendship goes for a six. Discipline, I am missing you in various chambers of my life, such as work, health and relationships.

You ask me who these non-friends are? Here. Let me name some of them for you.

'Non-Friends' of Discipline

- Each time you and I have an appointment for a walk in the park or an exercise session, **procrastination** along with **lethargy** make themselves readily accessible to me; leaving me without time-management and devoid of energy.

- When I open the fridge and find the chocolate mousse beckoning me, my **impulse control goes for a ride**.
- The same happens when I react with **anger** instead of taking a breath and responding calmly to a situation at work or at home.

Dear Discipline! I realise you are a learnt behaviour that needs practice; and, it is equally easy to unlearn you, if I fall prey to your new game plan of deserting me.

I have worked diligently with you to get my life sorted to the extent possible; and so, have been able to achieve whatever I have.

But of late, your new ambassador, **overconfidence** has been visiting me regularly. It gives me the false belief that I'll be able to get things done with last minute effort. Things either don't get done or get done shoddily.

With you by my side, I did my work systematically and got the desired results. You helped me look at long-term happiness, instead of short-term pleasures that are ephemeral.

Lack of patience, insufficient effort or hard work have made me get hooked on to **immediate gratification** and **quick results**. I find that I am constantly looking for a **short cut**; and that is hurting me.

How does this make me feel?

I feel **powerless** and **angry at myself**. I also feel **guilty** about succumbing to these unhelpful visitors.

Actually, Discipline, I am being unfair about blaming you totally for abandoning me. I know that I am accountable for it too.

I have made it easy for you to relax. Perhaps you wanted to test our friendship, by letting these non-friends of yours loose on me; and by succumbing, I let you down.

There are some chinks in my armour

Your so called friends find me easy prey:

- **when I am sad, anxious** and **over stressed**
- have had **lack of sleep**
- have **too much free time**
- when **I can't establish clear boundaries and say 'no' when I need to.**

Strangely enough it is also when:

- **I don't care for myself, or**
- **not love myself**
- **and hear strong voices of self criticism and judgement,** that make me give up
- **External unfair judgement that is critical and demeaning** weakens my resolve.

But dear friend Discipline, I have decided. No more of this!

I need to ensure that indiscipline, your alter ego, does not win.

How do I do it?

It has to be a well thought out plan. First, I need to accept that I am getting distanced from you and becoming vulnerable to counter forces. That has to change.

For this, I have to do the following. And while doing this, you, my friend Discipline, are not a burden but an ally.

- I am required to ensure that I am strong and protected from the attack by indiscipline
- I need to look after myself, physically and mentally
- Get enough rest and exercise
- Look at how I felt when we were together and how I am feeling when away from you. Ask myself why I miss you and what you do for me. Build my self esteem and self worth
- Handle my stressors effectively
- Explore and understand the context in which I allow myself to feel demeaned.

To do all this, I have to separate the problem from myself. Shift the focus from my identity to the context. Then I can cope better.

I cannot equate a slip-up of mine, with me being a complete write off. For example, just because I lost my temper, does not mean that I am a violent person. The two are not the same. I may have lost my temper on an occasion but that does not define the whole of me.

Understanding and accepting my sentiments and their triggers helps me work with them; and then I don't try and cover up for them. I am open to facing my internal issues and dealing with them. It helps me stay on track and opens up many choices and possibilities.

According to Mark Manson (in the article: 'If Self Discipline Feels Difficult, Then You're Doing It Wrong'), the classical approach to self discipline is:

'Self-Discipline = Willpower = Self Denial = Good Person'

This is how I would interpret this. If I'm fantasising about the sinfully delicious double cream mocha soufflé that I will scoop into after dinner but resist the urge with all the tenacity of my willpower, then I am a success, a good person who is a shining example of one who can exercise self discipline. BUT if I give in to the temptation then I am a washout as a good human being, one who has no impulse control, no command over his desires. And I end up feeling extremely guilty and pass a harsh and negative verdict about myself.

Quite understandably this is not sustainable.

This guilt merely breaks our self confidence and builds up tension and stress that eventually implodes and creates other problems.

What is sustainable in the long run?

I need to feel happy about embracing you, dear Discipline, because of what you are doing for me; and that good feeling is my reward. I can have all the right reasons for having you with me and they can get me started on the treadmill but I know that if I have to continue walking, I must feel good about it. By holding hands willingly with you and feeling validated for my effort with the results achieved, makes us long-term buddies.

We are on the same side, and you don't seem like a punishment for some wrong that I have committed. With you I am not denying myself, rather accepting and helping myself.

Next, I will ensure that I have a structure with which to work. I can hear your voice telling me what to do. Makes me happy—you warming up to me again.

- I hear you say that I need to set the much talked about **SMART goals**—specific, measurable, achievable, realistic/relevant, time-bound. For example, lose two kilograms in one month by walking for forty minutes each day at a brisk pace and following a reasonable diet.
- And when I achieve it, **reward** and acknowledge myself with something that makes me feel good.
- But while on the journey, it would be easier for me to stay off temptations, till I feel mentally strong enough to say 'no'; even if a fresh strawberry flan with cream is placed in front of me! Over time, I will develop new helpful habits and replace the unhelpful ones.
- I don't want to starve or deny myself all pleasures. So perhaps I can even look for other things that can give me happiness—like distributing chocolates to children who cannot afford them; volunteering in a library; doing story telling sessions; making hand-made soaps for a charity....
- Making others happy gives me a lot of joy, which in turn keeps me in a better mood to embrace you, dear Discipline.
- I could put up pictures of a fitter me on my cupboard to egg me on; talk to those who appreciate my goal and motivate me. Even if I slip up, say it's okay, carry on and remind myself why I began the journey.

- I need to be conscious of what made me slip up, what my internal hurdles are, take counselling help if necessary to help know and accept myself better. It could be that I overindulge in something because I am compensating for something else and I need to figure that out and deal with it.
- I need phone detox time so that I can do better time management to stick to my plan.

Word the goals in the present tense

I would like to word my goal in the present tense as if it is happening; and mention what it will make possible for me—not just 'lose weight'. This seems incomplete and somehow like an imposition. So I will say:

"It is giving me more energy to read, do gardening, be more productive, not waste time just lying around."

"It is giving me better sleep, helping me with health parameters, being lighter is helping me go on treks and climb."

"I am bending easily and cutting my toe nails without struggling, playing longer with my energetic grandchildren, using all the clothes in my wardrobe and not paying unnecessarily for alterations, feeling good about myself and happily puffed up (not too much) with a sense of empowerment." SO many benefits!

Cheers to our Friendship!

Yours Truly

PS – I find this quote inspiring:

> ***"Some people regard discipline as a chore. For me, it is a kind of order that sets me free to fly."***
>
> ***–Julie Andrews***

Introspection

1. What would be your interpretation of discipline? Do you think discipline is important?
2. Have you personally faced a problem with incorporating discipline into your life? If it is so then is it in a specific area?
3. Who are the 'non friends' of discipline in your life?
4. Of the tips mentioned above, which would you choose to help yourself?
5. What does discipline make possible for you?

6

Find a New Purpose in Life

Listen to Your Inner Calling

The pandemic set the internet abuzz with people of all ages posting videos of themselves singing, dancing, cooking, gardening, playing a musical instrument, reciting poetry.

You could sense the excitement and joy as they reconnected with a part of themselves tucked away in some unvisited, neglected corner in their beings. It was almost like a sense of coming home.

For others it was the thrill of a new discovery about their own self, about what they could do and had never done earlier. When the accessibility to the world outside shrank, the attention went inwards, uncapping the resource within; and uncovering the inner calling. As Tenzin Palmo said, "If you just follow your inner calling, then you just go ahead."

Bina was thrilled.

At fifty-two, she had never imagined becoming an entrepreneur. A homemaker, she was appreciated for her culinary skills but once the children flew the nest, the kitchen was visited only as a necessary duty. There was no real engagement, joy or sense of fulfilment in preparing the meals.

It was only during the lockdown that some neighbours turned to her for 'meal help' and so began a completely new chapter in her life. She found a fresh purpose in waking up every morning and checking out the orders and preparing accordingly.

"I have added a lot of new dishes to my menu. I realised that people need a choice and I taught myself. All the experimenting was both challenging and a lot of fun. Now I am confident. I enjoyed art even as a child. Today I find myself incorporating creativity in how I present the food and the special trays I create for festival gifts."

She connected with an inner calling. Her sense of self worth had taken a magnum leap.

Rakesh had been a successful analyst in a company.

With the new norm of 'work from home' and the travel restrictions, Rakesh found he had time on his hands and decided to learn the skill of making bonsais (small ornamental trees that mimic the shape of big trees).

"I now have a good collection of different varieties and looking after them gives me so much happiness. They practically talk to me. I can understand their needs and this is a wonderful feeling."

His enthusiasm is infectious. The question is, does it need a pandemic to 'uncork' a life force lying dormant within us?

What is 'normal' in life?

We all hoped that this situation would pass and we would get back to what we recognised as normal.

What does this normal mean for many of us? Work and family pressures can be all consuming at a certain stage in our lives. And that normal carries on for a significant period. It often gives us little or no time to peek into that deep well of life force inside us.

Normal is also the ticking of the biological clock. I have spent time with senior citizens who wake up one morning, post retirement, having recouped from sleep deprivation and taken their dream list of vacations; and wondering what they are going to do with the rest of the day; and the rest of their life.

One of them said, "I need a purpose. I need help to fill this yawning vacuum that threatens to engulf me." Mentally and physically healthy, the carpet seems to have been swept away from under their feet; and they find themselves standing on unfamiliar terrain, not knowing how to navigate it. Engagements outside the house deplete in number, children are engrossed in their lives and time hangs loose. As Friedrich Nietzsche said, "He who has a why to live for can bear almost any how."

Years ago, a person much older than me had advised, "Plan for your senior years when you are young. Life becomes much easier." Not all plans reach maturation but it is still useful to have a rough framework. Better still we could start the process of building a hobby or rekindling one, learn something new that we could use later, join an organisation that we could give more time to at a later stage, think of a project that we could do with like-minded people..." The idea is to try and make the transition to a new phase of life easier for us.

One of the outcomes of the long period of lockdown was to think about how to reinvent ourselves in our later innings, productively and happily. There is the serious business of planning finances, home and medical health plan. There is also the equally important aspect of mental health that we need to focus on. Said Viktor Frankl, "There is nothing in the world, I venture to say, that would so effectively help one to survive even the worst conditions as the knowledge that there is a meaning in one's life."

What will make us happy, content, feel worthwhile and help us look forward to a new day?

What is the Inner Calling?

There is obviously no generic one pill solution. Every individual needs to decide for himself or herself. Certain decisions are taken closer to the time depending on the circumstances; our geographical location, facilities available, our physical health.

The inner calling is not just about a profession. It could even be a great pastime. Many could be content relaxing, reading, travelling, socialising, watching movies, spending time with grandchildren. There are also those who might look/plan for something else.

Some interesting experiences of finding the inner calling

To share some more concrete experiences of those who found their inner calling:

Said a senior corporate executive, *"I have a good job, but I also had a dream of making a short film. I did not see it as a money-making venture but it was just something that excited me. One vacation I decided to attend a crash course in film making and that added so much quality to my life. I plan on making films for NGOs when I have more time."*

A very busy doctor, *who enjoyed his work but also loved painting, had not touched an easel in years. Till one day when he decided to join a workshop on charcoal sketching. It was the start of attending many such classes.*

This expression on paper and canvas was almost therapeutic for him in his stressful work; and today, when he has reduced his hours at the clinic, he holds exhibitions of his creations. He had found his inner calling.

In her thirties, *Sushma has a high profile career. For her the need to contribute to society has been an inner calling. "I want to set up an orphanage. It takes a lot of planning and getting the right people is certainly not easy. There are many legal aspects too. I've been working on all this slowly whenever I can find some time and hopefully it will become a reality."*

Another person says, *"My work and passion have taken me to many unique destinations and I've had some of the most strange and exciting experiences. I would love to share these but my writing skills are blunt.*

I've actually signed up for an online creative writing course and hope to put together my notes into a book at a later date. It will be an e-book."

A sixty-year-old lady *discovered a love for cycling and joined a group of cycling enthusiasts, most of whom were much younger than her. She found something that enthused her and alongside made new friends.*

Another gentleman *in his fifties joined several book clubs spread across the globe and this keeps him very happily occupied.*

Spiritual practice *is yet another area that many find peace and meaning in, especially once there is more time to devote to it.*

Isn't it amazing how so many people have connected with their inner selves? How about tapping into the being within you? And discovering a new aspect of you or reconnecting with a forgotten part of you; your inner calling!

Who knows, it could well turn out to be the journey of a lifetime!

> ***"Do what you have to do until you can do what you want to do."***
>
> **—Oprah Winfrey**

Introspection

1. Can you think of any inner calling that you have not paid heed to?
2. In life's hustle and bustle could you give this calling a little time—perhaps a song humming inside you; a story waiting patiently to be shared; a journey to a land that beckons; a start-up that needs to be started....
3. Do you know someone who decided to respond to an inner calling?
4. If you chose not to respond to your calling how would you feel a few years from now? On the other hand, if you did respond what would it make possible for you a few years later?

7

Finding Closure after a Failed Relationship

An interesting quote, attributed to more than one source, reads: **"It's not the load that breaks you down, it's the way you carry it."**

Most of us carry some baggage in life. But, for some, the baggage is heavier, depending on the particular life experience. Amongst those who carry the heavy load, some will neither crumble nor give up. Instead they re-adjust it, such that they can keep moving ahead with a certain amount of ease. **It is a choice they make.**

This, in other words, is the ability to find closure to issues that keep troubling the mind, so that one can move forward.

What does closure mean?

"I desperately need closure" is a sentence we hear often. It is usually a desire to close the door to a past unpleasant or unhappy experience and stop the painful memory from interfering with the present. In the case of the break-up of a relationship, it translates to a need to find answers to why it ended and what the future holds, more so if the person did not take the call for the break-up.

What do we usually need closure from?

It could be a memory or memories that evoke pain, fear, regret, anger and the like. The issues could range from:

- being betrayed by a partner or a trusted friend
- physical or mental abuse
- loss of a loved one, memory of a traumatic accident, loss of a job or something one associates one's identity with
- failing to achieve a desired goal
- intense regret at having either done something one should not have or not having done something one should have.

The feeling is on a replay mode, coming up and consuming the present. It hijacks peace of mind, productivity and freedom to simply be. Depending on the experience and what it is that we need closure from, the handling and the processing will be a little different. In this chapter, I will focus on closure from break-ups in relationships.

So can we hope to get complete closure?

However tempted I might be to say 'yes', I feel that often, a stubborn stain remains, even if very slight.

There may be moments when the mention or memory of it, causes a flashback. But if we have processed it effectively, those thoughts and emotions do not have the intensity to become a roadblock in our path forward because it is us controlling them now. Closure does not happen magically overnight. It is an independent journey along a path that we choose to walk and thus the outcome is more sustainable for us.

We may even learn to take a philosophical view of the episode and gain in wisdom.

Why do we need closure?

1. It could simply be treated as a painful or unhelpful thought, which will eventually fade away. But, the problem arises when it does not; and, keeps making its inroads into our current life.
2. Perhaps the most important reason to get closure is to get relief and release from something unseen, physically ungraspable, a thought that causes an unsettling feeling.
3. The freedom to have our thoughts and feelings in our controllable domain gives us stability. It also frees us from continuous tension, pressure and discomfort.
4. By regaining some degree of peace and equanimity, we also reclaim our bandwidth to be functional and productive in the present; and, not get stuck in the past.
5. And alongside, later, we do not regret losing our current invaluable time.

Closure gives us a sense of empowerment

If the trouble causing thought is caused by our reaction to a person, deliverance from it gives us a sense of empowerment. We cease being slaves to a remote control object; and, independently make choices that help us feel good about ourselves and about the future.

As we heal, we grow as a person; gaining maturity, attaining new insights into ourselves, in relationships, learning from our past mistakes and acquiring a wider perspective on life in general.

Suvarna had been, in her words, 'dumped' by her partner of nearly eight years. She was devastated and plagued by self defeating thoughts of not being good enough, of not finding any meaning in her life, having dreamed of her future with him.

She would obsessively look up his profile on social media and weep over his pictures looking radiant with his new-found love while she just withered away.

Despite being absent in her present life, he was controlling her breath, her tears, her very being.

Or, put another way, she was ***allowing*** *him or rather his memories, to do just that. She had relinquished all hold over herself and had morphed into being the proverbial lamb to the slaughter by self created images and doubts.*

"If I had lost him to an accident I could console myself that it is an act of destiny. But this is unbearable. I feel cheated and keep asking myself where I went wrong. How could he even do this? If only we had a second chance!

Now, I feel I can't trust anyone."

As humans we experience emotions of loss, anger, grief, self doubt etc. When dealing with difficult issues, we will go through phases of emotional turbulence where we question what has happened; perhaps even go through periods of denial, get angry and eventually accept the reality.

This need not be a linear progression. Emotions go back and forth. Relationships are complicated and multilayered. And, eventually, some form of closure is reached with the person acknowledging, accepting and finally addressing the issue.

It becomes a matter of concern when this process becomes very prolonged, with the person logging out of his or her 'normal' life and sinking into a form of 'victim mode', where he or she feels helpless to do anything. Some people feel the loss so intensely that they feel 'halved' when their partner leaves, without meaning or purpose in life.

So how did Suvarna eventually help herself?

1. She spoke to others who had gone through similar experiences and found solace and methods of coping. She spent time with people with whom she shared warm relationships and built new ones that gave her meaning in life.
2. Focused on her work and took courses in improving her skills.
3. Deleted her partner's number from her phone; and each time she felt tempted to check his status on social media, consciously did something else to distract herself.
4. She spent time on grooming herself to look and feel better; kept a pet and they gave each other company.
5. Finally, she changed her internal dialogue from saying that she was not good enough to saying that the loss was her partner's and not hers.

Once she felt stronger and got a grasp over her life, she could look back and see where she could have behaved differently in the partnership. This helped her in her future relationship.

How do we get closure?

No one answer applies to all. We need to find what works best for us and suits our comfort. We also need to remember to be compassionate with ourselves. To explain this, I will give a slightly different example. I met a mother who had become a mental wreck judging and condemning herself over not having brought up her child well, resulting in him not being able to hold on to any job as an adult and lacking all impulse control. When asked to revisit her past and think of all her actions or inactions that could have led to the current situation, she realised that she had done her best under the circumstances then, of providing him full support and guidance. It was an eye-opener for her and she gradually stopped blaming herself and regained her mental calm. She had been judging herself from her current circumstances which were far removed from the situation in the past.

As with many other emotions in our life, with closure too, we often look outside of ourselves to obtain it. The underlying belief is that the other person or a change in the circumstances will get us what we are searching for. This may never happen.

So do we continue to suffer? That choice is of course ours but depending on what we want closure from, the steps we take will differ.

Here are a few suggestions to deal with the break-up of a relationship.

- Do not get obsessed with finding closure. It will be like replacing the obsession of the negative thought loop with another pressure. It will take time, but we can help nature by taking constructive steps in dealing with it.
- With time, fresh memories and meanings are created and these gradually take precedence, allowing us to recover and heal. We try not to forcibly shut the door and instead patiently work on ourselves internally as much as possible.
- Stop seeking closure from someone else or from circumstances which may not change or give us what we are looking for. It takes away our own agency to help ourselves and generate our own understanding of the situation based on our beliefs which will help our healing in the long run. We consciously need to work on ourselves and our inner dialogue. Sometimes in desperation we almost seek alms from the other person involved, searching for answers, explanations or an apology. Some of us don't know how to apologise and everything in life cannot be explained. The desire to seek answers to questions often leads to more queries if the answers given are unsatisfactory or incomplete.
- If the other person wants to engage in a conversation, it is better if the dialogue happens after some time has passed from the breakup. Lurking within us is often a hope of meeting and 'making up' and we need to check for this because if the hope is dashed, it is like a double jolt. If the other person is unwilling to engage in any further communication, we cannot stay stuck; choked with anger, hurt, resentment and bitterness.

- An old remedy is to write a 'bye bye' letter, releasing all the feelings and wishing the person well in his or her future life and thanking the person for the happy times that may have been shared. It may never reach the other person but is a balm for the writer, giving a feeling of lightness and the bitterness is taken care of.
- Stop the 'What if' question that makes us float around in an illusionary fantasy world. Time cannot be rewound and neither can history be rewritten. The faster we accept reality the quicker we can work on it for our own good. We are able to find our strength and resources to move on and see productive outcomes from the experience.
- We need to reset our routine, take responsibility for ourselves, believe that we deserve a good life, spend time with loved ones, find new meaning and purpose in life, help ourselves grow in different ways, set healthy boundaries for ourselves and respect those set by the other person. In short, what we are searching for, the peace and equanimity, has to be generated from within us by accepting the present, acknowledging the pain inside us, and taking the steps discussed above to help ourselves.

If the negative feelings still continue to overwhelm, seek help from a counsellor.

> ***"There comes a day when you realise turning the page is the best feeling in the world, because you realise there's so much more to the book than the page you were stuck on."***
>
> **—Zayn Malik**

Introspection

1. Is there any past experience that continues to trouble you and you carry it like a load?
2. How would you help someone who needed your support in getting over a painful memory that kept coming back?
3. How would it help you to get closure from a repeated thought that is hurtful and overpowering?
4. What resources do you have within and around you to help you move forward from a painful experience?

8

Forgiveness

Giving and Asking to Enable Self Healing

Shubhra had been wronged; by the person in whose custody she had given her heart for safekeeping, with complete and no-holds-barred trust. Struck by this lightning, she reeled. With enormous effort, she recovered.

But she could neither forgive nor forget the person or the deed. Troublesome dreams, mental replay of times spent together, promises made and then broken, thoughts of how she would lash out at him if she met him, continued to haunt.

Then she met him; after years of no contact. Something snapped, releasing her from her own prison of pain, hurt and anger. She talked to him freely, breathed without tautness in her chest and went home to a night of wholesome, restful sleep.

She had set herself free. The situation had not changed. Yet, everything had changed for her. She had chosen to unburden herself of anger and resentment and forgive him.

What does Forgiveness mean?

Forgiveness means making a mental resolve to bring about a change in our attitude towards a person who we feel has wronged us. This is done by freeing oneself of thoughts of revenge, hitting back, wishing the offender bad, punishment, anger, blame, resentment. It means pardoning the person and setting both the receiver and the offender free.

According to Frederic Luskin, a psychologist and the head of the Stanford Forgiveness Project, *"The real work is when you've been harmed by someone you're close to and you work through all the conflicting feelings to go to a place of dignity and peace."* (Bruce Feiler, *The New York Times,* Sept. 25, 2015)

Forgiveness does not necessarily mean that things go back to a clean slate and there is total reconciliation. We can have forgiveness without reconciliation. It is a bonus if that happens too.

Sometimes even after forgiving, we go back to the earlier feeling of hurt and resentment. We then have to work on forgiving again. It is a process and does not happen miraculously.

Forgiving with Awareness

If two people have hurt each other, one can take the initiative of forgiving even if the other person takes his or her time reciprocating.

It is possible that the issue is with a person we are not in touch with or who is not alive. Letting go of pent up emotions, asking for or giving forgiveness in our hearts could be a way forward. We could refrain from talking ill of the person who has gone, to stop fuelling the resentment inside us. When seeking forgiveness from a person who is not with us, we could support a charity in the name of the person. It has to be something we choose to do and not compel ourselves because we have been told that it is the right thing to do. Forcing ourselves will not help in the long run because there will be no internal change inside us.

Then there are questions like, *"Why should I forgive?"* Or *"Does everything need to be forgiven?"* Or *"Isn't it better for our survival in the future to remember what wrong was done to us so that we are not open to hurt again?"* There could be other queries and reservations.

This chapter deals with the subject in a more generic way. However, one can say that forgiveness does not mean exposing oneself to future harm by becoming naive and trusting.

Awareness of what has happened—and may happen again—is worth keeping in mind like a lesson learnt. What we are talking about is not letting the anger or resentment make a nest inside us and corrode us.

How do you forgive someone who has wronged you?

- It is not easy but possible. It does not mean forgetting and excusing what happened; but it means not allowing it to strangle our current life.
- It also does not mean becoming close buddies with the person; but it does result in not allowing the sight of the person to irk and agitate us.
- One way is to put oneself in the other person's shoes, be empathetic and imagine how we would have reacted or behaved under the circumstances. Or, try and understand what made the person behave in that particular manner—without immediate judgement.
- It is easier to do this exercise with the passage of time, when the feelings are not as raw and we

are in a calmer frame of mind. It gives a different perspective to the one we were harbouring. It's like getting an alternate view, of what we had done that elicited a negative reaction.

- We may become more objective about ourselves and ask, "Was I actually that deeply wronged or did I feel wronged?" There is a difference.
- There would be situations when we had hurt someone and were forgiven. It is good to recall this and remember how it felt. The bottom line is to treat oneself and the other with compassion.

Joining a support group or talking to a mentor or counsellor often brings clarity and direction in what we should do.

How does forgiving help?

We no longer simmer in the pot of victimhood, waiting for redemption. We empower ourselves with the ability to tear away from the negative grip the other person has over us.

Forgiving is more about us than the other person. If holding grudges makes us feel negative and stressed then the reverse is also true. Letting go of grudges is beneficial for our physical, spiritual and mental well being. We do not have to wait for the other person to ask for forgiveness. We can do it within ourselves to unburden ourselves and let it go.

How the other person receives our pardon is not in our control; but it certainly makes us feel better and lighter and more in charge of our own emotions.

There could also be situations when we end up feeling hurt or hurting someone due to a miscommunication or misunderstanding. We might imagine motives behind a certain behaviour when in fact there are none. So before we judge someone's actions or words negatively, we need to be sure that our perception is not flawed.

Rajan and Akash were friends. One day they crossed each other at a distance on the road. Akash raised his hands in acknowledgement but got no response from Rajan who he felt was looking his way. This upset him and he brooded over what he felt was a deliberate act of ignoring him by Rajan. He in turn gave his friend the cold shoulder when they met next. The matter escalated till one day when Rajan asked Akash the reason for his 'strange' behaviour. On being told that he was the one who had started it, it came as a shock to him. He apologised for having missed the raised hand and explained that he had not even seen Akash.

So Rajan broke the impasse in the communication by taking the first step to clear matters and on understanding what had happened eased the situation by saying that he was sorry. Both friends felt much lighter. It was not easy for Rajan to broach the conversation. He was scared of being exposed to a cutting response but went ahead anyway because he valued the relationship. People are also fearful of forgiving and opening themselves up to being hurt again by that person. So we need to free ourselves of the emotional baggage, not necessarily to reunite with the person but to make life more pleasant for ourselves.

Asking for Forgiveness

Obviously, the question of seeking forgiveness comes up once we have acknowledged and accepted that what we did was wrong. Someone felt wronged and hurt by our action or inaction.

This might make us feel guilty, vulnerable and exposed and it requires courage to ask for forgiveness. There could be a chance that the person does not respond favourably but we apologise and ask for forgiveness for our own peace.

- The next step would be to truly feel remorse and express it to the person concerned. This requires time and introspection. The person feels respected, valued and understood. Whether the person is in a position to forgive is not for us to demand or judge. We simply need to do our bit.
- The initial step is apologising, followed by asking for forgiveness. When we genuinely feel and understand the pain that we have put the person through, the apology and asking for forgiveness has the depth that convinces the person.
- When apologising, this understanding needs to be put in words: "*I am sorry for having put you through the trauma of facing the land-sharks all by yourself. I needed to be with you so that you did not feel alone and unsupported. I was scared and chickened out but that is no excuse for not standing with you. Please forgive me and I want to assure you that in future I will not let you down and be there for you.*" Taking responsibility and giving assurance of rectification (our actions must reflect it) usually has a healing effect.
- Be specific in what you are sorry about.
- An interesting exercise of getting children sensitised to the idea of apologising is, for example, asking them, "You took away his ball and he cannot play.

How do you think he is feeling?" "What do you think you can do now?" Or "If he took away the ball you had got to play with, how would you feel?" "What would you want him to do?"

- We also need to forgive ourselves for what we did. Instead of labelling ourselves as 'bad' based on our action or inaction, separate our being and the act. "What I did was wrong." That does not mean justifying or finding excuses for what we did. We accept what we did was not right, try and see how we can make amends and move on.
- Some of us who find it difficult to verbalise our feelings and are comfortable writing, can gather our thoughts and pen them down.

Finally, if we express our gratitude to the person for apologising to us or for receiving our apology, we can take a step closer to healing ourselves, growing as a person and changing the situation.

For ourselves and hopefully for the other person too.

> ***"Forgiveness is not weak. It takes courage to face and overcome powerful emotions."***
>
> **—Desmond Tutu**

Introspection

1. Can you recall an instance when you consciously forgave someone or asked for forgiveness and received it? How did it make you feel?
2. What to you is the most difficult part of forgiveness?

3. If there is someone you need to forgive or seek forgiveness from and the person is not available, what do you think you could do?
4. Is there someone you don't want to forgive? What are you holding on to?
5. How would you feel if someone who had wronged you in some way came up and asked for your forgiveness?
6. Is there someone you need to apologise to and ask for forgiveness from?

9

Regret

Becoming Mindful about its Causes and Effects

If there is something to say, say it now;

If there is something to do, do it now;

If there is someone you can make glad and another less sad;

Do it now, do it now, do it now.

Do not wait until tomorrow;

For tomorrow may be just a little too late.

Many of us have learnt this at school. It talks to me, every now and then, as a reminder for not procrastinating about things I need to do so that I am not left with regret.

Regret. There is an unhappy ring to the word. It means feeling sad about something that one has done, or not done, or could have done better.

Studies have shown that there are more regrets about **not** having done something that we could have done.

What does one usually have regrets about?

Each one of us has some regret or regrets in varying degrees. It is an indication that we care and are engaged with life.

Regret about:

- having been unnecessarily harsh with someone
- not having spent enough time with loved ones
- having done something which caused hurt or harm to others or even to oneself
- not having valued or acknowledged those who have loved us and been by our side
- having used unfair means to get something at the cost of someone who needed it more
- having neglected our health
- having allowed ourselves to be treated badly
- having missed opportunities in life to do something we wanted to.

The idea is to live life to the full, in as much a happy, constructive and peaceful way as possible.

To make this idea a reality, an important element is to minimise regret.

If only—I wish I had—What I would do to get another chance—If only I could set it right—these are phrases that express feeling regretful.

All of them have one thing in common—a wish to rewrite the past, which as we know is not possible.

Sometimes, life experiences give us the perspective to see things in hindsight; and realise that we could have handled situations differently.

It is possible that we did not have the maturity then, took decisions according to what seemed right at that point in time and according to the resources then available; or, did not understand the implications of our actions and decisions.

There is also the possibility that we took the decisions consciously, even if it hurt someone else, because we simply did not care. And we regret it now.

What does regret do to us?

Regret is an emotion that we can do something about proactively to help ourselves; or, gradually let it consume us. It is a choice that will impact us in the long term.

What happens if we allow it to fester?

- We continue to sink into it deeper, berating ourselves about the past. It makes us acutely unhappy, with ourselves and the world because we cannot see and experience happiness.
- Self blame and inflexibility are other offshoots of obsessive regret. It may even result in self destructive behaviour and other health issues, both mental and physical.
- Inability to concentrate on current matters and move forward in life. It hampers our ability and confidence to make helpful decisions in the present.

A woman who divorced her husband over unjustified suspicions is regretful about her action and cannot get into a stable relationship because she is constantly lamenting the past.

Regret about having been in a long toxic relationship and not disengaging in time makes a man fearful about taking any 'risk' later. It might result in him hesitating to engage with life.

What can we do with regret?

"Being able to feel regret—the right kind of regret, which can be understood, worked through and can lead to remorse and

repair—is the strongest sign of a life meaningfully lived, of a healthy mind." —Moya Sarner in *The Guardian* on June 27th, 2019.

Trying to justify the action without feeling remorse/ repentance will get us stuck in the negative loop.

1. Acceptance

The initial step is acceptance of having made a mistake and genuinely feeling sorry and repenting it. And also understanding that a meaningful life can continue after that.

Rishika's regret of neglecting her parents in their old age was overwhelming her. "I prioritised my career over them. I did not visit them regularly. I could have insisted that they come and stay with me when I realised they were not being able to manage on their own.

They had always been there for me but I was not there for them. And now they are gone. I find it impossible to forgive myself for causing them so much hurt."

It was not possible to undo the past.

With therapy she gradually calmed herself and decided on taking responsibility for aged couples living in a home for senior citizens. She now spends time there during weekends.

She felt deep remorse and tried to repair her present. It was a balm for her troubled mind and helped in her hurting less, she felt less stressed and could go to bed, looking forward to the next day.

2. Moving Forward

Therapists believe that genuine remorse is a significant step towards moving ahead by exploring ways of doing something constructive about the situation.

Feeling regret and remorse is also an indication about what is important to us in life. It helps us set goals.

Rathin felt regretful about having wasted time and not being focussed on improving his communication skills by attending the workshops offered to him.

He now had clarity about his desire to improve his ability to communicate and was ready to invest time and energy into doing this.

- We need to acknowledge and identify our mistake and the specific feeling it is generating. Learn from it, apologise if possible, not repeat the mistake in the future and see if we can do something about it in the present to amend the damage.
- This is not to say that we will lead perfect lives in future and never make a mistake. We are human, work in progress till our last breath and mistakes do happen. But with increased awareness and a more mindful attitude, chances are that they will be fewer.
- This is the time to ask ourselves what we have learned from our past mistakes, are we allowing our regret to overpower us, what are we going to do about it in the future?
- Just as it is important to be compassionate with others, it is equally important to be compassionate with ourselves by experiencing the emotions gently and non-judgementally.
- Instead of negative self talk about past actions, look ahead, forgive oneself and replace the inner dialogue of, "How could I have done this?" or "Why did I not do that?" to "What can I do now?"

As L.M. Montgomery said, *"Tomorrow is always fresh with no mistakes in it yet."* We can allow ourselves that window to make a positive decision.

- We often judge our past actions from our present lens, based on suppositions. This may not be a complete or even a fair picture. Finding a background, a history and a meaning for the past actions gives relief and a sense of freedom.
- Sometimes we also overestimate the consequences of our past action or inaction, stretching them beyond realistic dimensions. *"If I had grabbed that job then, today I would be at the top rung of the Company."* Really? Any guarantee about that?

3. Being Grateful

Being grateful for what we have today and not undervaluing it, is useful for peace and equanimity.

Being grateful to our past for what it has taught us, to help us grow, is useful.

4. Healing

Regret, like other unhelpful emotions, can nest itself in our body—the shoulder, lower back, neck, sides of the forehead, stomach etc. causing pain and discomfort.

- There are techniques to release this tension in the body through Yoga and Mindfulness practices.
- Healing needs patience while working on ways/ projects to keep ourselves motivated.
- Regular self care, by consistently incorporating into our routine activities that we enjoy; physical exercise and mind calming methods.

- Interacting with people who help us and drawing boundaries with those who pull us back into unhelpful regret is important.

> ***"It's better to look ahead and prepare, than to look back and regret."***
>
> **—Jackie Joyner-Kersee**

Introspection

1. If a friend, partner or child were to come to you for advice about a deep regret they felt, how would you help them?
2. If given the opportunity to revisit a past experience you might have some regret about, is there anything that you could do about it now? It could pertain to someone else or even yourself.
3. Think of five situations regarding conversations that you have in your own mind about some form of regret, however small, and change the internal dialogue from 'If only' to 'This is what I can do now'.

10

Enough

A Compelling Word in Our Internal Conversations

What is Enough?

'Enough' is a concept. It is difficult to concretise it and distill it into numbers, a specific quantity or a measure. And the amount varies from person to person. 'Sufficient' or 'as much as required or needed' is an elastic term—stretchable or contractible.

Enough is a versatile word and has multiple uses. It permeates a variety of emotions. It is a powerful term in our internal dialogue. It is a resolve that we make for ourselves.

Let's look at three very common and important usages of this word.

1. Enough to be happy

Happiness is a feeling that is to be experienced. However, it has become a commodity that beckons—weighed against more money, fame, things, followers, deals, the 'best curated holidays' etc.

It has taken on the avatar of secret magic formulas that sit pretty on bookshelves; like the innumerable fantasies that we regularly chase:

- perpetual youth in looks

- the ever so desirable hourglass or six pack *dhamaka* figure
- the soulmate with whom we merge into foreverness
- 'spill-over' vaults in the banks
- power-packed performances at work
- progeny who will do us immensely proud

....the list goes on

We are the hunters, while our 'preys' are the elusive mirages that befuddle us. We need to conquer them, acquire them, own them. We seem to be so close...yet not there. And in all honesty may never be!

Yet...maybe...someday...

I admit that hope and a drive are great to keep us going, moving ahead. But should it be at the cost of dismissing and disregarding what is?

Being oblivious to the happiness present

The journey towards this 'maybe goal', towards more or better, can consume us so much that we are often oblivious to our **happiness** walking alongside us; feeling rejected, abandoned, waiting to be hugged, slowly dying to be acknowledged.

We have placed our own blinkers so securely that the beauty and comfort of our immediate surroundings are often invisible to us. And then, in all likelihood, when we get tired of running after this elusive happiness and tear off the blinkers—and seek the real happiness that was accompanying us—we find that we have actually lost it.

And then we are left with...?

Prathyusha, a woman in her forties, looked discontented. A stable job and marriage, two bubbly children, a solid roof over her head, annual family holidays to different destinations, a couple of close friends were not enough to give her the smile crinkles. Life, for her, was so ordinary, boring and routine.

She was seeking the spark of excitement. Only then would she be happy. And she waited... Her children grew up and left the nest; her husband, tired of her 'only ifs', found his own avenues of amusement and pre-occupation.

She is still waiting...to be happy.

Will that elusive spark of excitement, if and when it happens, be *enough* to make her smile? I wonder.

Is there enough money?

We have the minimalists who are constantly looking for things to discard, are not tempted by the 'mega sales' to stock up on whatever is available on discounts and are happy to live light. And there are the opposites, whose cupboards in every room are desperately obese, straining at every hinge.

Possibly, what many of us can never have enough of is hard money. How much is enough to feel secure, independent, safe, confident—with the bandwidth to splurge if the heart desires; to be a little reckless, even be magnanimous, philanthropic and generous, patronise the arts, set up institutions or an empire?

Our wants and wishes can be limitless.

A friend pointed out that we also need to calibrate our ego—to help us decide what is enough. Especially, if the enough is decided based on a comparison with those around.

"My friends are earning so much and I also need to be there." It can be a drive to work harder and also a trap in which we lose ourselves.

Prioritising...that's what is important. Where do we draw the line? It is a tough answer to give.

It also depends on how much money we are born into and what is 'normal' for us. But even in these categories, 'enough' is subjective. We must choose what makes us content; and do it sensibly. At some point we need to let go of our continuous hankering for more and enjoy what we actually have.

A quote attributed to Lao Tzu is, "He who knows that enough is enough will always have enough."

2. Enough is Enough!

And then there is the other enough—when we need to take a hard decision and say, "Enough is enough! No more." This enough too depends on the threshold level of individuals. So the amount of 'enough' varies. And the circumstances we are in, often determine what call we can take.

The choice is there, to decide how much we are willing to put up with, beyond which we take a stand, in whatever manner possible for us.

Rajat was a mild, good natured man who had become the butt of jokes in his office. He took this in his stride because he was uncomfortable with altercations. He found his solace in writing.

This continued for a while. Some colleagues had found in him a soft target, with whom they were having, what they believed, harmless fun. "He is such a sport. He does not mind our pulling his leg a little", was the response given when another colleague objected.

Soon the jokes became 'not so benign'. Rajat's reaction was building up but he had been quiet for so long that it needed courage to speak up for himself, though he was seething inside. He found his support in the one colleague who understood his plight and encouraged him to find his voice, saying he was by his side.

He finally found his voice.

During lunch one day he declared that he wanted to say something. Initially he was not taken seriously till his words penetrated the targets.

"I have nearly completed writing my book; and, my friend P..., I must thank you for being the epitome of generosity, by helping me create the character in my story whose only claim to fame is having enough fun at others' expense, to compensate for his own insecurity. I wish you enough self esteem to grow out of this."

"And my dear well wisher S..., you have shown me a unique aspect in communication—develop the knack of saying the harshest of things clothed in the sweetest of words. I hope your vocabulary and heart grow large enough for you to have the words and the empathy to reach out to people sincerely."

"And of course how can I forget my teammate G... From you I have learnt the subtle art of soft manipulation, so useful to you in life to get your work done by someone else. I would like that you get enough feedback to understand that people are not fools."

Rajat had drawn the line. ***Enough is enough. No more.***

3. Not Good Enough

Most of us have set ourselves standards, some which we are conscious of and of some we may not be. They provide helpful boundaries and can be useful regulators in how we conduct ourselves in various aspects of life.

Stepping outside of these makes us feel uncomfortable. An indication that something does not sit right. And then we need to step back and do what we need to, to feel comfortable.

There are also voices that we may have picked up in childhood or later in life; of *not being good enough.* Does this *actually* mean that we are not good enough?

Good enough for what and by whose standards?

Who do we need to prove ourselves to?

We may compare ourselves to others and feel inadequate. Our self esteem or self regard may be low, we may feel incompetent—these are signs that indicate that we feel we are not enough. It may even lead to various disorders and anxiety.

We may believe that we don't deserve support or help. It hinders us from trying something new because we don't feel competent enough.

Sometimes, even when we get a compliment, we are unable to accept it without suspicions. Self blame and constantly trying to please people reiterates the belief that we are not enough.

And we will never be, if we cannot help ourselves get out of this loop.

Unable to accept ourselves as *being enough,* if we keep trying extra hard to be like someone else, we are often neither here nor there.

We rarely* own *the 'good enough-ness' in ourselves.

This does not mean that we don't try to improve, grow, develop and flourish. To do this we first need to not berate, but accept ourselves; progress and learn in a way that is organic to us. There is the famous quote by Eleanor Roosevelt, "No one can make you feel inferior without your consent."

So we need to give ourselves permission to believe in ourselves; accept that we have our own strengths and also areas that need working upon; and carry on from there.

So at the end of it all where do we stand?

Where do we move from here?

A hope for balance, perhaps.

Experience enough trials and tribulations to keep us grounded and wise.

Enjoy enough love and happiness, to keep our peace, faith and enthusiasm alive.

Create a mindset of Enough so that we are not left craving, yearning, pining, coveting for that mysterious something, which, in any case, will fade into oblivion in the greater context of TIME.

> *"When it's time for me to walk away from something I walk away from it. My mind, my body, my conscience tell me that enough is enough."*
>
> **—Jerry West**

Introspection

1. Recall a time when you felt deeply happy and even the memory of it makes you smile. What made you so happy? Did you feel blessed with 'enough'?
2. What meaning does the word 'enough' have in your life?
3. How would you calibrate your ego regarding 'enough' in your life?
4. Do you agree that 'enough' is a resolve we make for ourselves? In what areas have you made this resolve for yourself?
5. Has there been an experience in your life when you found your voice and said 'enough'? How did it make you feel?

PART II
CONNECTIONS/INTERACTIONS

11

Saying No to Control in Relationships

By Self or Others

"If I was meant to be controlled, I would have come with a remote," is a line many of us have read or heard. I am not familiar with who wrote it but it is a very telling idea, especially in the context of the topic of this chapter. Let's start with a conversation between a wife and husband.

Wife: *"For your interview today I've chosen the linen blue shirt, dark blue trousers and the citrus cologne."*

Hubby: —*"Thank you. You make things so easy for me. What would I do without you?"*

Fast-forward to a few months later. The couple had been invited for dinner by relatives. As usual the wife chose the outfit for hubby dear—a brown and beige combination. It was a shirt she had bought for him.

Wife: *"You look so good in this. I have something in similar shades. We will be a colour coordinated couple. Can't wait to hear the comments."*

Hubby: *"Was thinking of trying out the maroon kurta that Nihar* (his brother) *gave me for my birthday. I have never worn it in all these months. This is a casual occasion when I could actually use it."*

Wife (miffed): *"I just thought we could have some fun. Nowadays you don't seem to have faith in my choices."*

Husband was in a quandary. The 'help' he had appreciated had taken on the avatar of being a controlling force. Should he or should he not follow his own wish; and in all likelihood face a petulant spouse for the next few days if he did what he wanted to?

Are you waiting impatiently to know what he finally decided? He had learnt the art of skilful negotiation.

"Sure we will have fun when we meet our friends next week. Save your dress for then. Nihar will be there tonight and he will be happy to see me wearing the kurta."

Initially unaware of the manner in which he was being controlled and manipulated, hubby could sense a feeling of suffocation. He realised his freedom was getting compromised—being constantly monitored, checked and watched.

To understand what was happening, he decided to take Counselling help.

A Counselling Conversation that helped bring clarity

Counsellor: *"What I am hearing is that you are experiencing a feeling of loss of control, even in regular mundane matters. This understanding is recent for you. Could you think back and tell me if you had felt like this even as a child?"*

Hubby: *"Now that you ask me, yes. Sometimes I felt overwhelmed even as a child. I could not explore or experiment like my friends did. It was all done for me. My family would even breathe for me if they could."*

Counsellor: *"What did you feel?"*

Hubby: *"In hindsight, I think my feelings were mixed. I enjoyed being pampered, but I definitely missed being me. I missed the excitement and happiness of doing things on my own, feeling a sense of real achievement, being mischievous, getting into trouble, making mistakes. I had been denied that freedom."*

Counsellor: *"And today somewhat similar feelings are overwhelming you. You are feeling helpless, powerless and you want to break free."*

Hubby: *"Yes. I wish to exercise my choice and not be made to feel guilty or justify myself at each step."*

Counsellor: *"And who will do that for you?"*

Hubby: *"I realise it has to be me but how do I do it?"*

Many of us have experienced it at some point; the feeling of claustrophobia and the need to break free from prying eyes, emotional blackmail, pressurisation, demands, from the feeling of being blamed and made to feel guilty.

Sometimes we even become slaves to our own, self-created pressures; and the need to exercise continuous self control, whereby we throw all spontaneity out of the window, becoming mechanical in our lifestyle.

But we will not discuss self created pressures—for now.

How do we know we are being controlled?

Here are some common ways; there may be many more:

- Being threatened with dire consequences, if we do something against the wishes of the controlling person.

- Feeling cornered, gas-lighted, watched and blamed for things that go wrong, which we are not even responsible for.
- Becoming aware that there is unusual sweetness when something is needed from us.
- Constantly feeling criticised while nothing good is acknowledged.
- When the other person feels there is a need for us to 'change'.
- When the other starts controlling us through finances.
- Being constantly answerable to the other person.
- Victim card being played by the other person and creating a drama over small matters.
- Interference in and micro-managing of our actions by the other.
- Segregating/separating and isolating us from those we are close to and can trust.
- Controlling who we talk to or mix with.
- Not accepting a 'no' from us and disrespecting our boundaries.

Why do we need to be in control of our lives?

It is natural to want to be in charge of and have a say in our own lives. We cannot get even a pet to do things against its will. We all love the freedom of making a choice and having our wish respected; from whether to have a cream cracker or a ginger biscuit with our morning tea to much greater issues. It gives a feeling of well being.

It is a different matter whether we are able to acknowledge, accept and take responsibility for our choices.

Why do we sometimes want to control the lives of others?

The problem arises when we take away the others' choices and wish to control their lives.

Why do we do it? (We will not address psychotic disorders in this chapter).

Some reasons are:

- Insecurity—of losing control and becoming unimportant, low self confidence and self esteem.
- Inability to trust—either out of suspicion or lack of faith in the ability of others.
- Deep seated fear of things going wrong without our input, management and control.
- Anxiety/inability to relax.
- Seeking attention, a desire to be in the limelight.
- The belief that we can do it best or we know best what needs to be done.

How do we stop being controlling?

1. Usually it needs someone else to point out that our behaviour is oppressive and controlling. It is the receiver who has to bear the brunt of our high-handed and bossy attitude.
2. If we are introspective, we can sense that our behaviour makes people uncomfortable, distant and wary; making us feel alone and unwanted.

The loss of genuine companionship and warm ties might make us want to change. Asking for feedback about ourselves from people who matter to us, can be helpful.

3. It helps to understand why we are doing it, where our internal insecurity, fear and limiting beliefs stem from; and then work on them with help.
4. We gradually realise that we cannot control everything in life, even if we try. Changing our own unhelpful behaviour is possible.
5. Handling our own anxieties and becoming calmer helps in changing our driven behaviour pattern.
6. Taking a step back and seeing where our controlling behaviour has got us, how it has affected those around us and doing a debit-credit analysis gives us useful insights.
7. "How would I feel if someone was trying to control me?" is a good question to ask ourselves.
8. Observing others who have better relationship management techniques is helpful.
9. In the short term we may get our way but over the long term we lose abiding relationships and the rich inputs of different viewpoints. Changing our internal dialogue by consciously deleting words related to control helps us change our thoughts also.
10. Looking at uncertainty not as a threat or something fearful; and instead, taking it in our stride as a fun challenge, where we can think of creative ways of handling it and dealing with it as a team.

11. It helps to be conscious of our intention and what we hope to achieve at the end of the conversation. This makes us mindful of how we communicate.

How do we break free from being controlled?

1. The awareness of being controlled; and the resultant unease, must be strong enough for us, to want to claim our place in the sun and say "Enough! No more! I want to have a say in my own life and I need you to back off." Of course, our language and technique of standing up for ourselves will differ depending on who we are dealing with. It is a skill we need to develop.
2. Travelling from the awareness of being controlled, to the desire for autonomy; to executing it and expressing it; is the journey towards breaking free.
3. We also need to learn the methods of assertive communication—being firm and clear, but not aggressive. This needs consistency, patience and a calm approach.
4. If we choose to put up with a certain degree of controlling behaviour, we should be able to examine and explain to ourselves why we need to do it.
5. There may be situations where we do not have the scope to take a hard decision of opting out or being vocal about our needs.

   In such cases, we try and work on other areas—like focusing on our personal strengths, developing skills to make something of our lives, learning ways by which we can stay insulated from the provocation of controlling behaviour. And understand that even this is a choice we are making.

6. Focus on what is important to us, be confident of what we choose. Then how others respond will be inconsequential. We can decide not to give our mind space to relive painful controlling behaviour experiences.
7. It might help to try and understand what makes the other person behave in a certain way. If we can find particular triggers in our behaviour that sets the other person off, we can be mindful about it and try and minimise it.
8. It is a useful practice establishing boundaries in relationships that get intrusive; expressing how we feel and what we need without blaming, and knowing when it is prudent to leave the situation.

There is also the interesting area of needing to be in control of every aspect of our **own** lives. That can also create immense stress and anxiety since things often do not pan out the way we plan.

It has been wisely said that though we cannot choose or control the external circumstances we can decide how we respond to them.

"Our anxiety does not come from thinking about the future, but from wanting to control it."

—Kahlil Gibran

Introspection

1. Look at yourself objectively from the eyes of those you interact with regularly. How would they see you—controlling or comfortable to be with?
2. Think of those you spend time with. How do you feel when you are around them? Do any of the feelings of being controlled listed above resonate with you?
3. Which are the steps you would like to take to protect yourself from being uncomfortably controlled where you lose your own agency?
4. Are there any areas in your own life where you create self pressure by trying to control every aspect of it? How do you think you can relax and let go a little, doing your bit as far as possible and then simply letting things happen?
5. Was there an instance where you stood up against someone trying to control you? How did you do it and what did it make you feel about yourself? Also, how did the person trying to control you deal with you after the episode?

12

Setting Boundaries in Relationships

An Exercise in Self Care

A cuddly child was a great temptation for adults around her to give her a squeeze. She did not enjoy it and used all of her two year old form to firmly tell them off by shaking her index finger in a clear 'no' every time she felt them getting too close.

Sometimes she would 'allow' them a hug if they asked her permission and she was comfortable with it.

It was a fascinating lesson for me, about how a baby could intuitively express her need for boundaries with firmness and dignity.

Boundaries—both physical and psychological—are 'limits' set to differentiate what belongs 'inside' and what belongs 'outside'. They are a way of satisfying basic human needs to establish one's safety, stability, security and identity.

How do boundaries help?

To answer this let us look at the reverse; that is, what happens when they are **not** set.

Richika was unable to set any boundaries with her boyfriend. Due to her lack of autonomy and being blindly entangled and enmeshed in the relationship, she could not free herself from his manipulation.

Intellectually she understood the reality; and, emotionally felt disrespected and trampled upon. But she had a very hard time setting a boundary and sticking to it.

Facing a burnout and seething with anger at herself, she finally decided to distance herself; and deny him his unreasonable demands. With help from her counsellor, she decided on her 'rekha' with him; and others too.

It was a tough journey but reaped her much benefit, of regaining her self confidence and self esteem.

Abhay was a cauldron of churning emotions. His personal space and time was being constantly encroached upon by his supervisor at work; and he had been unable to draw the line between work and personal life. It was the realisation that he was losing his family's love and respect for him; and his own failing health, that woke him up to take a call and show compassion for himself.

Setting boundaries is actually an act of kindness to oneself and self care that is essential in the long run for a healthy, balanced life.

Setting boundaries is about you; not the other person

According to Priscilla Claman in the *Harvard Business Review*, January 13, 2021, "Boundary predators rely on their power and authority—and your passivity—to get what they want. It's up to you to push back, by understanding how to create boundaries and maintain them...."

So the story is not about the 'other person'. It is about **you** relinquishing personal autonomy and facing the consequences for that. We cannot change the other person.

We can try and ensure that we communicate our feelings firmly and—if disregarded—decide on the further course of action, knowing that it is for us to exercise a choice.

Being 'boundary deficient' impacts us in the short and long term:

- Unnecessary and time consuming arguments
- anxiety, feeling violated
- vulnerability to manipulation
- strained relationships
- feeling pressurised
- compromising on opportunities that help us grow and be more productive.

Protecting psychological and physical boundaries

Carving out and protecting psychological and physical boundaries gives us a sense of space and freedom, a comfort zone, a place to breathe freely without being buffeted painfully by judgement, unreasonable demands, feeling disrespected and impinged upon. It helps us to look at our options in a given situation and decide, based on what feels right for us, instead of being overwhelmed by views of those around us.

It is a protection from being encroached upon. It makes people aware of our needs and how much can be expected from us. Over time, it evokes respect and establishes that we cannot be taken for granted.

A gentleman served a delicious meal, but would want his guests to leave by 10 pm after dinner. He was an early riser and needed his sleep time respected. Initially some did not take him seriously and tried to push him and trivialise his boundary. Instead of getting into an argument, he merely went off to his room after bidding them goodnight, quietly enforcing his boundary.

The lesson was learnt.

Once we realise how our personal boundary setting is helpful for us, we also become more sensitive to—and aware of—not encroaching on the boundaries of others. We also do not personalise issues as one of 'rejection' or feel victimised if the other person sets limits. It helps in building relationships that are mutually respectful.

What stops us from setting healthy boundaries?

Often, we are not even conscious of our right and need to have boundaries. And it becomes a habit to keep compromising even though we are unhappy.

Many of us carry a baggage of not being good enough; and so, are afraid of rejection, if we demand that our requirements are met.

There could be other impediments to setting boundaries and securing them. Given below are some of them:

- Fear of conflict
- not knowing how to speak up or stand up for oneself
- the need for acceptance and approval from others at all costs
- the threat of losing a job/position
- lack of self confidence
- low self esteem

How do we set boundaries?

1. The first step is the awareness of what we are—and are not—comfortable with.

Does our action, in the face of a difficult situation, make us feel empowered or does it buy us only a short-term respite?

It requires us to listen to ourselves and be in touch with our feelings. And—in a mindful way—be present in the moment; give ourselves the space to breathe, think, scan our choices and then take a call.

There is no generic template for personal boundaries. Each person defines it based on individual relationships and circumstances. We need to be conscious of our feeling of comfort and create them with words and matching behaviour. There are laws regarding privacy, property, personal safety and defamation to name a few but we need to establish our own defining lines of boundary in regular interactions.

2. We can set personal boundaries that do not involve any other person.

What it does need is discipline and awareness. It could be setting personal limits to the number of drinks we consume; how many helpings of sweets we have; not watching television for more than a certain time period etc.

3. When working with people at home or at work, it is more effective to have a conversation and set the boundaries in a collaborative way.

This gives everyone a sense of inclusion and the decision is not forced.

If a new agreement has to be decided upon, it is best to get clarifications and know what we are getting into. And it is important to make our position clear at the outset to avoid future misunderstandings. The tricky part here is to develop the skill to manage ourselves and our emotions during the conversation.

4. Also if we need to say 'no' to a request, we need to learn the skill.

A colleague with whom you don't want to sour your relationship, asks you to exchange a particular class timing with her on a continuous basis. It is inconvenient and annoying for you.

You need to be setting boundaries and yet not say a 'no' straight away. The answer could be, "I am ready to help you out today. We need to sit together and rework your class schedule to avoid this situation in future." The message that you are not ready to oblige in the future is clearly communicated in a polite manner.

5. Boundaries are not set in stone but not free flowing either.

A reasonable boundary allows flexibility when the need arises, but that must be a free choice. The person cannot be pushed to succumb. As caregivers, for example, we also need to set boundaries for our wards/children/patients.

Boundaries are open to being opposed. Occasionally, we need to allow room for a little negotiation provided we reiterate the rules and preferably in the same discussion.

"I understand that you need to stay out late tonight and, that is okay; but the rule still stands at 9.30 pm, for other weekends."

6. Some boundaries outlive their utility or are not suitable for changed circumstances. We need to rethink those and decide.

To end, I want to share a story that is very insightful.

At a home for rescued animals in Africa, run by a dedicated animal lover, visitors were invited to visit the large fenced area of a white lion.

They could go inside with the handler; and were each given a long stick, which they had to hold at an arm's length by stretching out the arm.

The logic was that the lion too was aware of personal space. It hugged the handler by standing on its hind legs and putting its front paws on the handler's shoulders.

But, while it was comfortable with **only** *the handler going close to it, it had been trained to respect the distance between the stick and the visitor, as the visitor's comfort zone!*

"When you say 'yes' to others, make sure you're not saying 'no' to yourself."

—Paulo Coelho

Introspection

1. Have you ever experienced a 'boundary predator' who has used your 'passivity' to bully you? Of the suggestions listed above, which one would you use to help yourself?

2. Is there any area where you would like to set a boundary but find it difficult to? What stops you? How does it make you feel? What would you like to do about it?
3. Think of a time when you consciously drew a boundary when encroached upon? What did it make possible for you and how did you feel about yourself?
4. Is there any boundary that you have become rigid about due to habit and find it difficult to be flexible? What has been the outcome of it?

13

Relationships

Resolving Issues Before It's Too Late

"Don't go to bed angry" is an advice that has often come our way; sometimes with the addition "...with yourself, with someone else or with the world at large."

Going to bed while still angry, often hampers sleep, creates unrest inside us and detracts from our peace of mind. Over time, it also has other ramifications which we will not dwell on right now.

Working on one's Relationship with Self

Times can be difficult and unpredictable as the world recently experienced with Covid 19. The uncertainty of how the situation will unfold makes one hesitate to make plans. But, one can take steps with what is in our control.

We can work on our relationships. To start with... with ourselves. We could begin with acknowledging and accepting what is making us angry with ourselves, forgiving ourselves, learning from it, see if there is something we could do about it and move on.

I am reminded of Martin Seligman's concept of positive psychology, whereby we can flourish in our lives and focus on what is life-giving.

Working on Relationships with Others

A while ago, I was gifted with an insight from a young man in his mid twenties. He was on a difficult mission and the situation appeared to be closing in on him. "I did not want to die with a troubled mind—with unresolved issues; with people who mattered to me at some point in my life."

"So what did you do?" I asked. "I had my mobile phone and what I could do was record messages for those I wanted to settle issues with. Say what I was feeling; not with anger, but with a mind to resolve the matter."

"What counted was the relationship and not the issue. And that is what I did."

Fortunately, he received timely help, but a very valuable and meaningful learning had intuitively come to him early in life.

The story did not end there. He also recorded messages for those he wanted to thank; to tell them that he loved them and acknowledged them for the role they had played; and the significance they had in his life. This covered those younger than him, his peers and those much older.

Verbalise feelings with loved ones

We often forget or hesitate to verbalise love, affection and gratitude to those who matter the most. "What is the need to spell it out? It sounds so put on. Isn't it taken for granted that we love them?" is often the logic given. Reams of love notes and messages are reserved for the courtship period and the early days of a romantic relationship. And then it is 'taken for granted'.

Dale Carnegie said, "When dealing with people, remember you are not dealing with creatures of logic, but with creatures of emotion..."

I recall another person's experience. She had never found the 'right moment' to thank her father for all the aspects of life he had introduced her to; love for nature, yoga, equanimity, honesty; everything she held so dear. Till one day, when he fell ill, she realised that she might lose him and live with the regret of never telling him how much he meant to her; and thank him for giving her a life of joyful abundance, that had helped her tide over many trying situations.

Finally, telling him what she felt, gave her tremendous peace and joy. She could see the same joy reflected in his eyes and smile.

Would we like someone to tell us that we were important in his/her life? Would we feel freer if a person tried to resolve an issue that had been troubling a once close relationship we had shared? It is possible that the relationship would not go back to where it was at one time, but perhaps the sting could be mitigated.

If the answer is 'yes', how about taking a step in that direction with someone we care for, if we haven't already.

It might require some preparation with a shift in our paradigm and approach.

> ***"We cannot solve our problems with the same thinking we used when we created them."***
>
> **—Albert Einstein**

Introspection

1. Spend a little time thinking about your relationship with yourself. Do you like yourself and enjoy your own company? What answers came up for you?
2. Is there anyone you would like to say something to—thank or resolve an issue with? Someone you have taken for granted and not acknowledged? Have you been taken for granted by someone and not been acknowledged for being there for the person? How do you feel about it? What would make a difference for you?

14

Personal Freedom

Securing while Managing Relationships

> **"You can muffle the drum, and you can loosen the strings of the lyre, but who shall command the skylark not to sing?"**
>
> **—Kahlil Gibran**

Here are a couple of situations:

"I just cannot control my child anymore. Earlier he would do as I said but now, at four, he has a view about everything—food, clothes, sleep time, handwriting, games... We were so obedient as children. I dread to think of what will happen when he is older."

Rewind—Do we actually remember how we behaved as infants? How did we feel being constantly controlled?

"Today I feel angry with myself for being so weak. I understand now that he was trying to control me with emotional manipulation. Knowing that I craved his company he would deliberately not take my calls, making me desperate. Meeting him would be at a time suitable only to him.

Yet, when I was working he would call me to prove his power over me since I would take the call. When he wanted something he would be sugar sweet, another method of mind control."

She broke free of his mind tentacles when her free spirit finally revolted and reclaimed space and personal freedom.

"My happiest memory is not the birth of my child but the feel of my own house keys in my palm to enter and exit as I wanted. I was suffocated giving explanations to my in-laws about where and why I was going out, what time I would return and be made to feel guilty if I ate elsewhere."

The desire to control, often in the garb of concern, alienates and chokes the person.

The key theme in the anecdotes above is the clash between the need for **freedom** and the desire to **control**.

The need for Personal Freedom

'Control' is a word loosely used. And we often take it as an entitlement to exercise power over those we are close to, including our very environment. It is almost an unconscious act. If we are exerting it, so can the other person, and it can turn into a manipulative power struggle.

The truth, as we all know, is that any relationship brings with it constraints and commitments—in varying degrees. And the sooner we accept this, the better for us. It goes both ways; and, how each person defines personal freedom varies.

Right from birth we are conditioned to some constraints on our freedom. Meal timings, Nursery schedules, rules of behaviour and it continues. We are trained to exercise restraint and be aware of responsibility even when we are free and no one is actually monitoring us. If we go off the track and are caught, there are consequences.

So when do we miss being free? The obvious answer is when something we are accustomed to is denied to us or when we are pressurised into behaving in a manner not natural to us.

Certain relationships by their very nature are hierarchical and some are partnerships between equals. Both have expectations which make dents in our freedom.

Willing compromise is smooth. Compromising a little grudgingly, but deciding it is prudent, by looking at the greater picture, is acceptable.

But modifying or crushing the yearning for personal freedom without being able to object becomes unliveable. Autonomy and choice are natural needs. Once a person is old enough to think and reason, there is a desire to be involved in decisions regarding himself or herself.

We also need physical space and mind space, where certain thoughts, experiences, feelings, memories are just our own.

Freedom we seek in relationships

I spoke to people of various ages asking them what 'freedom' meant to them in this context. These are some of the responses I got:

Not feeling trapped; somebody not trying to change me all the time; being accepted as I am.

Not being constantly answerable for whatever I do; freedom to simply be.

Overpowering and obsessive love can be suffocating.

Being financially free so that I am not dependent.

Being able to speak my mind; not having to regularly listen to the words 'I'm allowing you'.

Not be compelled to follow superstitions and rituals that I don't believe in; freedom to say 'no'; freedom to be HAPPY...

There are many different ways of looking at personal freedom.

The next question is:

How do we carve out our personal space and gain our personal freedom?

1. Start with ourselves in the intra-personal space

Strange as it may sound, **even our own mind can rob us of our freedom**—rigidity, obsessiveness, low self esteem, lack of self worth and negativity in our own thoughts and attitude can chain us and this may get reflected in how we interact with others.

A new bride was having a trying time adjusting to the superstitions followed by her in-laws. Those imposing these rules on her were equally trapped in their own minds, complicating their own lives at every step—and did not perceive it as anything unusual, causing chaos in someone else's life.

One can argue that they had the freedom to believe in the superstitions, but the problem arose when they imposed it on someone else.

So the start is to free ourselves—from our own prejudices, insecurities, inflexibilities, unreasonable expectations, feelings of entitlement and the like. And the first step towards this would be to become conscious of these hurdles inside us, causing problems in interactions.

We can seek help to identify them if we cannot recognise them on our own.

2. Being sensitive to others while seeking our own freedom

Asking for personal freedom requires providing the other person freedom and space—be it a child, friend, partner, colleague, employee or parent. Even while making personal decisions we need to keep in mind how it will impact the other person.

Freedom involves taking responsibility and that can be liberating too if it is aligned with our values.

A father took a conscious decision to reject a lucrative job offer because it would impact the future of his children. It was a choice he made while exercising his freedom, keeping in mind his responsibility as the father.

Asking ourselves how we would feel if we had someone breathing down our back is a useful barometer to check in with how we are conducting ourselves. Being aware of another person's needs helps us become more compassionate and adds more meaning to life.

"To be free means that one has the burden of making choices and decisions. And in making those decisions and choices, we are responsible for both our own and others' freedom." —Ron Breazeale PhD, in *Psychology Today*, January 13, 2021.

3. Cooperating with others for mutual benefit

Helping each other grow, growing together and giving each other comfort would be a few of the ideal tenets of a nurturing relationship that allows space and personal freedom. Use dialogue and negotiation to handle issues to reach a workable solution.

If there is a continuous attempt to control, therapists suggest trying to become an observer and not personalising the matter. "It is their problem, not mine." This gives some relief and space to respond based on one's own beliefs and needs.

There is no ownership in any relationship—even with our own progeny. However, if there is complete dependence of one person on the other, be it financial, emotional or physical, the logistics may get altered. There is no obvious ownership but there is often a tilt in the balance of freedom, towards the provider.

4. Not expecting others to change

People adapt to each other with time but if the intention is to change the other person there will be repercussions.

Constantly trying to please the other person and pretending to be what he or she is not, is also not sustainable.

"My wife was aware of my lifestyle before marriage but a couple of years later she wanted me to change it to something entirely different. I told her that she knew me earlier too and her answer was that she was sure she would be able to change me."

Value the relationship and not take it as a right. A good nurturing relationship with a partner, friend or child allows freedom—the freedom of security, support, comfort, love and companionship and the freedom to be weak and vulnerable too. It is precious.

"Relational freedom, paradoxically, involves sacrificing some freedom to experience it. Yet, what we lose in some freedoms is easily made up for with the addition of other

freedoms." —Jim Taylor PhD, in *Psychology Today*, August 23, 2021.

> ***"...for you can only be free when even the desire of seeking freedom becomes a harness to you, and when you cease to speak of freedom as a goal and a fulfilment."***
>
> **—Kahlil Gibran**

Introspection

1. Aggressive independence may be damaging to a relationship. How would you keep a balance between securing your personal freedom and also making your partner feel needed and wanted through inter-dependence?
2. How important is your personal freedom to you? Are you also sensitive to the need for personal freedom of those around you?
3. Think of a time when you felt suffocated because your personal space was being regularly impinged upon? What was your response? Was it helpful? Is there any other manner in which it could have been handled?
4. In your own mind is there any repeated unhelpful thought loop that robs you of your freedom to be happy? What can you do about it?

15

Parents & Adult Children Relationships

How Much is Too Much to Expect?

Let's start by looking at a conversation between a Mentor (M) and a Client (C):

C: *"I feel very guilty making any demand on my son. He is our only child and I don't want him to feel burdened."*

M: *"What do you feel guilty asking for?"*

C: *"Oh, I don't ask for anything material. Fortunately we* (the parents) *can manage comfortably with what we have; and he is doing well too. But sometimes I ask him to call us at a particular time. Even when we go across (overseas) to meet him, I don't want to intrude."*

"Occasionally he comes home for lunch when we are there, so that we can go out for a meal together; or he takes us out in the evenings. He is so busy that doing anything extra, I feel, is a pressure on him."

M: *"You have been a career woman all your life, looked after your family, brought up your child and your parents lived in another city. Did you too feel pressurised if your parents asked you to make some time for them—call them, visit them?"*

C: *"Even if occasionally I did feel pressurised, I still did what I needed to. But times are different now. He is burdened* *with so many tensions, work related responsibilities. I feel scared that it will affect his health. There is also all this talk of giving the children space. I feel confused, about how much is too much."*

M: *"Do you believe that he has some responsibilities towards both of you too? What would you, as parents, like him to do for you?"*

C: *"Just be around a little more, for us. I know that is not possible physically all the time, but if he could visit us more often, even for a few days* and *talk to us more, so that we don't feel cut off. Nowadays we talk once in three weeks or so."*

M: *"Has he ever asked you not to make any 'demands' on him as you put it? Or told you that it causes him anxiety?"*

C: *"No, that he has not; but I can see that he is constantly on call, rushed for time, meeting a deadline; and that is what makes me hold back. Even when I do call, there is often an interruption when he has to attend to an urgent issue; and our conversation gets cut. Sometimes I feel I am trying to justify his behaviour for my own mental equanimity."*

M: *"And how does that make you feel? Holding back, not telling him that you want him around a bit more, that you would like him to call you more frequently, be more a part of his life and vice versa?"*

C: *"Actually, I feel distanced and sometimes I do feel hurt. I realise that I end up making polite conversations as I would with an acquaintance. So many things happen in our lives, but the effort of remembering them and conveying them does not happen. I feel, why bother, he is not really interested."*

M: *"And what does that finally result in?"*

C: *"Probably trying to make peace with the fact that my job was to bring him up, nurture him and prepare him for life. And then let him go."*

M: *"I can sense that you want to say something else."*

C: *"Perhaps what I am saying is that I cut the string of the kite and let him fly. I did not make him grounded, conscious of his responsibilities towards us, his parents. In giving him his freedom and being consciously non-intrusive, we drifted apart. The problem is mine.*

"We are now in the late autumn of our lives. Somehow we figure low in his list of priorities. It never seems the 'right time' to make time for us. There is always some overarching matter. I know that if there is some emergency, he will be there; but it seems a pity to wait for that."

M: *"Let me ask you how you feel, having made yourself available to your parents, when they were getting on in years?"*

C: *"I feel a lot of peace inside me. I feel happy too, because memories of the time spent together; just talking about mundane things, reliving small incidents that happened years ago, enjoying and cherishing our time together, is a source of strength for me.*

"I know that they felt wanted, needed and cared for in their sunset years too. For myself, I don't live with any regret of not being there for them. There were situations when it was not easy carving out the time, but I knew they were waiting for me. That made me feel special too."

M: *"Have you told your son that you both wait for him to call or visit you and that you miss him when he does not?"*

C: *"No, I have not in so many words. I have told him that we are very happy to see him. But I don't tell him my needs."*

M: *"Do you think it would be a good idea to do that?"*

C: *"Yes, I suppose it would be. Perhaps I am scared of his response, of his trivialising my feelings."*

M: *"Do you think it could be an assumption on your part?"*

C: *"It probably is. I don't know. But yes, if I say it then I would know that I have expressed my needs. The rest is up to him. I know that I don't live with guilt and regret regarding my role towards my parents. He has to decide his choice once I tell him what we miss."*

Parents and Adult children often drift apart, unintentionally

The conversation quoted above is representative of many such situations, where parents and children gradually become strangers to each other; because of a lack of regular meaningful communication; non-expression of genuine needs, not prioritising the time and effort necessary for nurturing a relationship or taking things for granted. I am sure many more points can be added to this.

There is a phrase that I came across relating to what is called a psycho-social issue. The acronym is PICA—Parents in India, Children Abroad. Psychiatrists say that issues of depression, anxiety, loneliness, feeling of abandonment are often faced by such parents.

During and, as an aftermath of COVID 19, many of these issues became heightened because travel was a challenge and the miles separating the parents and the children seemed insurmountable—mentally and physically.

Counsellors have had cases of children living in far off lands, contacting them for help for their elderly parents living in India. In a certain section of society, Counselling as a safe place to talk about their fears and feelings and discuss ways of coping, is now fairly acceptable, for the senior generation facing this situation.

Strange as it may sound, it does happen that parents wait for the children to call and vice versa and there is a sense of '*abhimaan*' or sense of hurt on both sides. A young girl who had gone overseas to study was lonely, stressed with work and unused to looking after her regular work of laundry, organising her meals or contacting a doctor when she was unwell, felt even more burdened. She needed assurance and support. In a bid to show that she was independent and could look after herself, she would not tell her parents her troubles and yet when their calls were not as frequent as she desired, she would feel even more lost. It led to a misunderstanding though in actuality both the parents and the child wanted to be in close contact. It was only later, when a family friend who had met the daughter, informed the parents that they needed to call their child more that the true picture emerged.

What we understand from this story is the importance of communication, keeping in regular touch and not waiting for the other to call if the relationship is very important for us. If ego, as we understand it in common parlance, gets in the way, it can play a lot of mischief.

Some tips to prevent the drift in relationships

It is important to figure out why this drift happens, so that preventive and curative steps can be taken to deal with emotional pain and hurt.

Here are a few steps that could be taken to make things better:

- Technology has given us many options for communicating. Use them freely and set aside at least one specific time every week, suitable to both. If there are grandchildren, talk to them too on a regular basis.
- Regular exchange of pictures and videos of events in each other's lives. A young mother shares videos of what her children are doing, with their grandparents, three to four times a week; so that they feel included in the joyous experience of the children growing up.
- If there is a phone call or a message that is sent from either party, acknowledge it and say you will get back the moment you can; and actually do so. If the matter is urgent, then it should be mentioned in the message or the voice recording.
- It is advisable to know the emergency contact numbers of both parties who can be contacted, in case the party is unreachable for some reason.
- When talking, try and minimise complaints or advice. It puts people off.
- Share family news so that there is a feeling of connectedness.
- Keep each other informed in case of travel.
- Visit when possible.

- Surprise gift packages are always welcomed by recipients.
- On special occasions, it is fun to send messages through videos where family and friends participate.

Each family will have its own unique inputs to decide what works for both, the parents and the adult children.

> ***"Make time for each other, not as a task that one is compelled to do but because not doing it means missing out on something precious."***
>
> **—Anonymous**

Introspection

1. If you are living far away from your parents/children or even living in the same house, how much time do you set aside to spend with them every week—over the phone or in person?
2. Are you happy with the closeness in the relationship if you consider it important? Can you think of different ways to keep the connection tighter, adding fun and care so that each one looks forward to the next interaction which is uplifting in nature? The reverse would be complaining, demanding, nagging and constantly advising.

16

Compromising and Settling for Crumbs

Does it Lead to a Sub-optimal Life?

A friend of mine recently had her cataract operation. What she said was very telling. "It is amazing how much better I can see. I had forgotten what good vision was and had settled for a slightly blurry picture for so long, thinking that was normal."

Yes, of course, I told myself. How true. In so many spheres in life we find ourselves compromising; accepting lower standards over a period of time, almost unconsciously—from ourselves and from other people.

Sometimes we don't have the energy to fight for quality. So, even while knowing it is available, we settle for peace at the cost of quality.

Compromising reduces the quality of life experiences

At times we simply get into a 'chalta hai' (it will do) mode and that becomes the norm. It could be some very mundane, routine activities, like setting the table for a meal and eating food there. I had become lazy and would take the plate of food and sit on the bed or on a chair, while watching television. Or, I would just eat in the kitchen when eating alone. Laying out the table with a mat and coasters seemed like too much effort.

This was till I visited my octogenarian aunt, who was living by herself, with no full time help. I found her eating lunch at the table, complete with a table mat, cloth napkins, a jug of water and of course, the food. It was a very simple meal that I was invited to partake of, but the entire experience was so much richer and satisfying, than just dumping the food on the plate and eating it anyhow!

I realised that I was compromising and had settled for the '*chalta hai*' syndrome, sacrificing the complete joy of enjoying a meal in an aesthetic and pleasing manner. The beauty of the experience had been lost. I was neither doing justice to the food nor was I valuing the effort of the person who had cooked it, even if the cook was me. I had lowered my own standards regarding myself; it had nothing to do with anyone else.

Settling for Crumbs affects quality of Relationships

In relationships too, it is the same story. We often fall into the '*dreary desert sand of dead habit*'. The truth is, that deep inside us, we know whether we are happy or not. Often we are just conditioned to accept and adjust to whatever is doled out to us. We neither give the best of ourselves to a relationship nor do we expect much, often settling for crumbs instead of sharing the entire cake.

It is like getting used to the taste of dry bits of sweet, packaged flour sold as cakes; missing out on the moist, soft, butter flavoured original bakes.

Compromising per se, is not necessarily wrong. It works well when all parties concerned give each other an honest hearing with respect and make concessions to arrive at a consensus for the greater good.

The trouble happens when one party feels totally disregarded, and yet is accepting less than the basic standard.

Why do we settle for less than the minimum?

- Fear of conflict, criticism, rejection, change and of the unknown
- Not being confident about our own ability to manage outside the familiar terrain
- Financial insecurity, societal pressures
- Insecurity regarding the future of the children

These are some of the reasons I've come across. Often, it is easier to complain than to take the trouble to do something proactively, to improve the situation.

Even when it comes to growing, thriving and actualising our own potential, fear of failure, inertia or simply ambling along in a comfort zone act as impediments.

How not to settle for crumbs

- The awareness that one is over-compromising is important. That way we do not suffer from any illusions.
- Nature has programmed us with the ability to detect our discomfort; if only we take the time to listen to ourselves and observe our feelings.

- We need to change our mindset, to say, *"I deserve a better quality of life and will do what I can to achieve it."*
- Instead of giving in and quietly accepting anything and everything, we learn to speak up against what is unacceptable.
- It is not easy but it is 'learnable'. With practice one finds the right words and the courage. If necessary, we can even learn at training programmes or from a coach.

It might sound a bit dramatic, but most of us are un-introduced to our own reserves and tenacity to survive and prosper. We can bake our own rich plum cake with soaked raisins and nuts to enrich our lives. The quantity of nuts and raisins will vary depending on our situation but it will be better than crumbs.

We can enhance the quality of our life by adding new colours, gaining new knowledge, learning and sharpening new skills, revisiting and upgrading what we were good at and seeking out all the resources available to us. There may be risks involved and pain at not achieving what we set out to do; the results of our effort may not be visible immediately but there is the satisfaction of having tried and not living with regret of nothing attempted, and nothing gained.

We have the choice to avoid over-compromising

Initially, our speaking up might antagonise the other person, who is used to behaving callously. But over time, if we persist, we will be heard.

- If we are not heard, we know that we need to look at other avenues open to us.
- If something is not working right, we don't have to wait for the other person to take a call. It is our life and we need to take responsibility for it. We can take professional help to see if we need to handle things differently and put in the effort from our end.
- In certain cases, if unsure of our rights, we might even need to take legal advice so that we can be on firm ground if the need arises.
- Whatever decision we take we need to think it through, understand its impact and have a back-up plan. It gives us self respect and, over time, respect from others; including, even if grudgingly, from the person who was doling out the crumbs.

Whether we do or do not settle for crumbs is a matter of our choice. Sometimes we choose to or are compelled to and learn to make peace with it.

But what nobody else can control is whether we are authentic and the best that we can be—towards ourselves and those we interact with. That has its own rewards and satisfaction.

> ***"I don't understand people who say, 'I don't give this to people, or that to people; because nobody gave it to me before...' But that is exactly why you should give it! Because you know exactly what it feels like not to have it! And you never want another person to feel the way that you did!"***
>
> **—C. JoyBell C.**

Introspection

1. Have you got used to blurred vision in some compartment of your life? How would cleaning the lens help you? What do you think it will make possible for you?
2. Do you ever hear yourself say, "I used to enjoy...." or "I used to be good at..."? Why do you say it in the past tense? What can you do about it now?
3. Is there any part of you that feels neglected and needs some love and care? How about giving it some attention?
4. Can you focus on any two issues that maybe acting as impediments to lead a complete life? What can you do about these?
5. Think of three areas of your life where you have never compromised on a basic standard. What made you stay steadfast in these areas?

17

Dealing with Generational Family Conflicts

Resolving and Finding Peace

"Pain travels through family lines until someone is ready to heal it in themselves. By going through the agony of healing you no longer pass the poison chalice onto the generations that follow..."

I read and re-read these lines that I came across (attributed on the Internet to different sources) and they resonated deeply.

Family legacies come in different packages. Amongst many happy and inspirational stories, lurk some family conflicts that are painful, destructive and caused the great divide. It even becomes a question of family honour to abide by; for a stand taken by family members, way, way back, who had crossed swords, literally or otherwise.

Generations later, the individuals may not even know the details of the family conflicts; or hear only the version propagated in a particular line of the family. Often these are versions curried and garnished with spicy details with the passage of time and fertile imagination.

Analysing this a little deeper, we might notice other biases too that we subconsciously harbour inside us. Biases based on what we may have absorbed from our environment—racial bias, caste bias, religious bias, biases based on superstitions and blind belief...the list goes on.

Man is born free—unfettered by any prejudices. Socialisation is the process through which we form opinions. We always have the power of choice—to observe, process and decide for ourselves what action we can take.

What is family conflict?

In this chapter, we will look at discord and strife with the extended family; and also families without blood ties. Family conflicts—between cousins, with aunts and uncles and their families or between two families that had once been close. It could be a situation where, over generations there has been tension, no contact or protracted legal battles.

Take this case of four siblings from a well to do family.

It was a time before the partition of India when the migration of the younger generation to more attractive pastures in the west was not as prevalent.

The father had visions of his two sons and sons-in-law working together in a firm that he had set up. Each had his own expertise and the initial years went well. The business prospered and the coffers expanded. Till one son decided that he wanted more.

Trust was compromised and the family conflict started; when realisation dawned that things were anything but transparent. With proof in hand, one brother walked out of the business and the family home with a suitcase; and ventured off on his own.

Matters were not taken to court since the family reputation was at stake, but the ties amongst the family members had been guillotined due to the family conflict.

Of course, word got around that something was amiss, but there was never any public declaration of it. The two brothers would not attend social or family functions together and their children never met. The 'poison chalice' was passed on to the next generation.

The cold war continued for several years. Then something interesting happened. At a certain point, the families lived in the same city and the social circle they moved in, overlapped. The child of the brother who had walked out, heard from a friend, that he had an older cousin who was a heartthrob with the girls in his college. Curiosity overcame him and he asked his parents why he had not met the cousin.

And so began the dilemma for his parents. Should they disclose the details to their child? Just because the father of the cousin had wronged his siblings should the children suffer?

What probably helped in taking a decision was that the concerned brother had no interest in the family money and had built his own life. He had cut the umbilical cord cleanly. The cousins met without baggage and built a relationship.

Years later, the child of the cousin, who had heard whispers of the family rift, wanted to verify what he had been told and visited his uncles' father to hear his story. All sides could put their versions on the table, but the matter remained where it was; a part of the family lore with no real bearing on the present.

When the opportunity presented itself, a call had been taken by the wronged brother to let history remain where it was meant to be—in the past; and he had allowed the living and relevant present to breathe and grow healthily. In the process, he possibly healed himself and stopped the chasm from deepening further.

What are the usual causes of these family conflicts?

History is witness to innumerable famous family feuds. The causes are often repetitive.

- Physical or mental abuse; over controlling behaviour
- Strong feelings of betrayal, jealousy, unfair treatment
- Property disputes; sibling rivalry
- Uneven division of responsibilities whether it be in business or looking after the elderly, chronically ill family member
- Misunderstandings which could be through unclear or inappropriate communication; breach of trust
- Unacceptable romantic or sexual liaisons; conflicts over differing values and beliefs.

How does one handle these family conflicts?

1. To begin with one must want to try and end the conflict because closing it genuinely means something to us.

The sustained bitterness can be corrosive; and especially, if we are trapped into taking a stand on a matter not of our making. Then, we almost become slaves to it, since we are not exercising our free will.

By doing a debit-credit assessment of the situation, we can make a judgement about what to do. Of course, we do realise that a strife implies two sides; and that both parties must be on the same page for the attempt at a resolution.

2. It helps if we mentally break the mindset of 'us' and 'them' and move towards 'we are a family' or 'we can be on the same side'.

Coming from this faith and spirit, it will translate into our behaviour too and make our attempt at reconciliation more genuine.

3. Generational malady is like a still stagnant pond where the water is getting putrid.

To move on and refresh the water, we need to gather facts about the cause of the family conflict and be convinced about the expected outcome being worth the effort.

Once convinced, we could make the first move at reconciliation, instead of waiting for the other person.

4. The idea is not to try and change the other person's beliefs.

The focus is to move on despite the past animosity. If the goal is to convince the other person about your side of the story, chances are that the meeting will be a non-starter.

5. **In case the past trigger question does come up, consciously decide to allow the person free space to speak. Listen and, if you have a different perspective, agree to disagree; and reiterate gently that the idea is to move ahead.**

Be mindful about not getting provoked and allowing feelings of anger, hurt, betrayal, revenge or control to distract you. It is not about taking the matter personally. The method in which you communicate—choice of words, tone, volume will also have an impact.

6. **Detachment and observation are two important tools in this endeavour to resolve family conflicts.**

Be like a detective, objectively examining what is happening between the families concerned; the unhealthy and maladjusted characteristics in relationships. Simultaneously, observe helpful interaction techniques in families with healthy and buoyant relationships.

7. **Holding age old grudges amongst families, which often have nothing to do directly with the current generation, perpetuating hate and conflict, seems like such a waste of precious energy and valuable mind space.**

Today we are the custodians of upholding our larger family peace and goodwill; and also with families with whom we share ties over generations.

> ***"Seeing unhealthy patterns in your family and deciding that those patterns end with you and will not be passed down to future generations, is an extremely brave and powerful decision."***
>
> **—Tiny Tot |** ***TheMindsJournal***

Introspection

1. Have you experienced family conflict that has been passed down the generations? If you have then does it impact you in any way today?
2. How will it affect future generations in your family? Do you feel it is worth it for you to do something about it?

PART III
INTERACTIONS & ATTITUDE

18

Every Life Experience Counts

10 Tips on How to Handle Tough Times

A recent hospital stay, for a surgery that I had delayed for a long time, brought with it a bouquet of life experience benefits; other than the expected results of the procedure. I received nuggets of advice, each with a different perspective and a different learning.

Even the voices of discouragement that I experienced, regarding the pain and the possibility of the surgery going wrong, made meaning for me.

The messages got me thinking, about what they meant in the bigger scheme of life. I realised that they could help me handle the tougher surprises that were bound to come up over and beyond this planned procedure. So, I journaled them into a 'thought' and 'it's implications' format.

Here goes…

1. ***"Once you have taken an informed and well thought out decision, don't keep second guessing yourself."***

"It leads to confusion, stress and is pointless. You cannot control everything."

Choose to have faith in the person whom you have chosen for the job; and enjoy the comfort of those who are by your side. Affirm to yourself that all will go well. It cuts out the negativity about the life experience.

2. "Just think of your stay as an extended vacation where you will be pampered."

"Room to yourself, an array of persons available to you at the press of a bell, food brought to your bedside, someone to even give you a sponge bath! So many perks!"

How you see the life experience depends on your perspective—whether as a punishment; or, as something that has positivity in it for you as well; and needs to be taken in your stride—graciously.

3. "You have invested a lot of money in this surgery. See it as an investment."

"If you were to invest your savings, you would look to maximise your returns. So do everything possible to get the best out of it."

Invest your time, energy and money wisely and then do a regular follow up before, during and after the actual investment, to see that things are moving on track. Be with it and see it through.

4. "You've been an athlete. Just remember the stairs in the stadium that you went up and down."

"Awaken that person inside you and take it on!"

Focus on your resources—within you and those around you—and ask for help if needed. Don't underestimate yourself.

Also remember, that support often comes from the most unexpected sources.

5. *"Chant this mantra whenever possible. It has a protective power and gives inner strength."*

"Do deep breathing to relax and use mindfulness techniques to calm yourself." "I will be praying for you and remember that your loved ones, seen and unseen, will be with you."

Have faith in whatever or whoever you believe in, to hold your hand. The power of the unseen hand of a greater energy, the love of dear ones, gives one a feeling of safety and comfort in any experience.

The ancient practice of *pranayama* and the vibration of mantras being chanted, create an inner pool of calmness. It is the inner well that helps us when in pain, confusion, stress or anxiety.

This helps us in taking better decisions by de-cluttering our minds and also gives us relief when under pressure in any life experience.

6. *"It appears to be a big challenge now; but once it's behind you and you look in the rear view mirror, you will feel that you have achieved something."*

"Think of the future benefits; and time will take care of the healing."

Think of long-term benefits from the particular life experience and not short-term fixes. Life cannot always be on a fast forward mode. We have to respect time, the mother tincture. It will heal and reveal.

7. *Bring in some humour. "Opioids given as painkillers may give you the feeling that you are in La La Land!"*

Find humour in life. It helps alleviate a lot of things. Don't take yourself and your difficult life experiences too seriously. They tend to overwhelm you and sometimes you start feeling lost. Accept that situations are not always in our control. You are at the driving wheel of your life. Take charge of it, look at the options open to you and then make an informed choice that you are comfortable with.

8. *"Think of others who have gone through and are going through tough situations."*

"Talk to them about their experiences and you will find different coping methods."

You are not alone in your struggles. Each person, a king or a pauper, faces challenges and learns to cope. So will you and this too will pass.

9. *"Think of what prompted you to take this decision—obviously you hope for a better future."*

"Focus on that and the current challenge will seem worth it."

Allow your hopes and dreams to motivate you. Each little step will take you closer to it. Just keep moving.

10. *"I know someone, who, when she was told she would be hospitalised for a while, took an immediate decision to do a few things."*

"She upgraded her upholstery and curtains in her room and drawing room; bought new mugs for serving tea to her guests, when they would visit her on her return; got herself a facial, pedicure and manicure; and on the day of her surgery, went into the operation theatre with her full make up done!"

However funny this might sound, it displays a certain spirit and zest for life. Take care of yourself. Howsoever tough the going be, always put your best foot forward.

Face situations with courage and confidence and be careful not to expose your vulnerability to all and sundry.

> *"We cannot change the cards we are dealt, just how we play the hand."*
>
> —**Randy Pausch in *The Last Lecture***

Introspection

1. Think of a tough decision that you have had to make in a difficult situation that you faced. Think of the steps you took and the outcome.
2. What did it demand from you?
3. What lesson did it teach you for handling future tough situations that might come up? How has it better prepared you?
4. Is there another tip or tips that you could add to the list given above in the chapter?
5. Which of the learnings talked about in the chapter resonated with you the most and why?

19

Gossip

A Compelling Human Need or an Avoidable Distraction?

A sixteen year old was being interviewed for the position of School Captain. The senior administrators wanted to test his leadership qualities. They asked him his opinion on the worthiness of the other students who had been shortlisted for the post.

His response was, "I reserve my right to not discuss my classmates." The boy refused to fall for the bait to gossip or pass judgements about his peers. He displayed strength of character and was selected for the spot.

Curiosity—the compelling need for gossip

Gossip—discussing people who are not present on the scene of the conversation—is one of humankind's favourite pastimes. Being absent, persons can neither verify nor negate what is being said about them.

A dictionary meaning of gossip is, 'casual or unconstrained conversation or reports about other people, typically involving details that are not confirmed as being true.'

"No one gossips about other people's secret virtues."

—Bertrand Russell.

Behind it all is curiosity, the compelling need to know. *"The things most people want to know about are usually none of their business."* —George Bernard Shaw.

For those gossiping with the information, it is their need to tell.

'Deals' are struck about: "I will tell you *this* if you tell me *that*." Information is power—social power and the power to control. There are groups within groups, carved out on the premise of who knows what.

Much like the well known game of Chinese Whisper, a story that might be a simple, benign pasta dish, after a few ears and tongues, becomes hot and spicy Szechuan pasta in chilli oil!

Celebrity gossip hits headlines, is splashed on every form of social media. There are detailed descriptions, as if the person writing was privy to being an eyewitness. PNPC—*para ninda para charcha* (salacious talk about other people) is the phrase for it in Bengali.

I sometimes wonder what birds tweet about, when they are in groups. Or, for that matter, what animals do? Do they discuss the lives of other animals?

Probably not. They, in all likelihood, have more urgent and pressing matters to settle. So much to learn from them!

Types of Gossip

Some studies show that gossip can be classified into three categories—neutral, positive and negative. It is also said that gossip is an integral part of communication and helps in information sharing, bonding, community building and plays a role in staving off loneliness.

Neutral Gossip

This could mean simply sharing news about someone who has visited an interesting place, is unwell, has had an addition to the family, has changed his or her job and the like. It remains neutral if one is sure about the intent of giving the information—not judgemental or malicious, not revengeful or disrespectful; and, not with the intention of causing harm or gaining some personal interest. It can have a positive impact if the receiver of the information takes positive action, like giving the person who is unwell, information about a good doctor To call it gossip would mean that the person who shares the information might like to show that he is in the know of things and in this way draws attention to himself. It could also be the manner in which he shares the information—for example, if the information to be shared is about a person having gone on a vacation, the way in which it is said could have bits like, "He has gone to Europe *again* within a year. Wonder who is funding it?" It is no longer neutral gossip.

Positive Gossip

Gossip may be seen as positive if, for example, it reiterates accepted social norms which are for the greater good. For example, there could be discussion within a group about a person, who has the habit of playing one person against the other, in the group. Chances are that the message will get back to him. He becomes aware of the consequences of his actions, such as being rejected by the group; and so changes his behaviour. There is a positive outcome from the gossip. Saying something good about a person is also positive.

Negative Gossip

Negative gossip is unverified information based on assumptions, coloured by judgements, sharing further of something shared in confidence; it is salacious, unkind and often downright mean (for example, negative comments on the person's looks, family background, financial status etc). In other words, it has no productive impact; is a huge waste of time and is usually hurtful. In the garb of showing concern, it is often simply loose talk. It could stem from being envious; or, to prove that "I am superior."

Frank A. Clark has an interesting take on gossip. He says, *"Gossip needn't be false to be evil—there's a lot of truth that shouldn't be passed around."*

Some Risks of Negative Gossip

Negative Gossip damages reputations, which are difficult to salvage; often impacts the target of the gossip psychologically; alienates people; and in the workplace, leads to 'group-ism', breach of trust and stressful situations.

There is complete disregard for a person's privacy. Even little children are not spared. And as they grow, certain embarrassing stories about their childhood become the fodder for entertainment, when families meet.

Are they ever asked how they feel about this?

Of course not! And the labels stick. Supposedly funny stories about him or her wetting the bed for a longer duration than the norm, being a bully in the Nursery school, taking a desk partner's fancy eraser in Class Two without asking; and such like. Infants grow to become adults, often carrying the tag socially and emotionally.

I remember an incident when a woman, supposedly affectionately, recalled her nephew's childhood habit of going to birthday parties and quietly eating chunks of the birthday cake long before the birthday boy had the chance to cut it and he also helped himself to the goodies on the table. This had earned him a rather mean nickname that she disclosed. Of course it was totally inappropriate to discuss this, on the part of the woman, causing the young grown nephew in his thirties, huge embarrassment. What was far more painful for him was that it was said in front of his son who hero worshipped his father and this story drove the child to tears.

Apart from the fact that indulging in negative gossip is a nasty habit causing hurt and pain, considering the amount of time spent on it, it is a loss of constructive and productive time and does nothing for the growth of the participants. If anything, it 'de-enriches' people.

In his book *The Art of Communicating,* Vietnamese Buddhist monk Thich Nhat Hanh has written, *"When we say something that nourishes us and uplifts the people around us, we are feeding love and compassion. When we speak and act in a way that causes tension and anger, we are nourishing violence and suffering."* So the choice is ours.

Becoming Mindful of Negative Gossip

The following points could sound like taking away all spontaneity and becoming a digitised robot. Initially it might appear to be so. With practice and sincere desire, it is not an effort.

1. We could just become more aware and speak with sensitivity and compassion. "How would I feel if the same is being discussed about me?" is a useful question to ask oneself.
2. Obviously it is not in our control to monitor what others around us are saying. And we cannot become a social recluse by staying out of all groups or avoiding all the people who indulge in gossip. But we can try and steer the conversation to another topic or refrain from participating in any way.
3. Asking ourselves if we would be comfortable, saying what we are, in front of the person being discussed, has been advocated as a useful method.
4. Communicate mindfully—be aware of what we are saying and what its impact will be.
5. Thich Nhat Hanh talks of a simple way we can do this. Just take an in and out breath consciously, before pressing the send button on a message; or saying something on the phone. We can do the same when the impulse to share juicy news pushes us. The breath is a powerful pause for allowing our judicious and compassionate self to get activated.
6. Another method is to ask ourselves the intention behind sharing the information. Over time we gain respect when we are known for not being party to idle gossip.

A Spanish proverb is good to remember when we are consumed with the desire to gossip. *"Whoever gossips to you, will gossip about you."*

"To All My Dear Friends & Relatives... Just remember me in your prayers like you do in your gossip."

—Rajesh Menon

Introspection

1. An acronym often shared on social media urges people to THINK before sharing any information—keeping in mind if it is **T**rue, **H**elpful, **I**nspiring, **N**ecessary and **K**ind. Which of these do you consider when sharing any news?
2. Have you ever experienced any false information or loose talk being shared about you? How did you feel? Did anyone object to this negative gossip?
3. What would you do if some negative talk about a person, that had no basis of truth or evidence, was shared by someone with you?
4. Take a moment to think of those you spend a fair amount of time with. Do you come back enriched after the conversation or is it mainly gossip about people? What is your contribution?

20

Harsh Words Hit the Person

Not the Problem they Face

Remember the song 'Words' by Bee Gees. The refrain is:

> *"It's only words and words are all I have, to take your heart away."*

What if I were to think of the opposite:

> *It's only words and words I always have, to shred your heart away.*

Sounds rather dramatic, right?

Words are potent and powerful

Words are invisible; they can leave indelible scars. They are potent and powerful. It is in our power to use them as we choose. Much has been written about the impact of words. They have energy and need to be used mindfully.

Eight-year-old Feroze was a marvel with any musical instrument. The beats and tunes flew intuitively through him. Yet, the math class was a nightmare and he struggled.

The attitude of the teacher did not help. She mocked him in class, as she distributed the corrected answer scripts; and called him 'dumb' and 'stupid' for repeating an earlier mistake. What this did for Feroze's self esteem is not difficult to fathom.

Brainless, embarrassment, disappointment, dud, wicked, failure, useless, worthless, slob are other such insults often meted out to children, by those in authority. When repeated frequently, the little beings invariably internalise these harsh words as defining them.

At an office, an employee was told, "I should have invested in a monkey. It would perform far better than you." And yet another was sarcastically ticked off with, "I didn't realise that such losers qualified from such reputed business schools."

Fortunately, the first recipient of these harsh words had the courage and the confidence to stand up to the boss; who, realising the gravity of the situation, tried to make amends with an apology. But not many are made of this mettle; and, the fear of losing the job or getting a bad appraisal, makes them swallow the insults and carry them around; sometimes even believing that they are indeed worthless.

Harsh words not necessary to correct behaviour

Individuals who use such insensitive and harsh words, have obviously never learnt the basics of communication. If they were to ask themselves two simple questions, "How would I feel if I was treated like this by my seniors?" and "What is the intention of this dialogue, will it help?" they would speak differently, and use words more constructively.

So what do we take away from these incidents?

While addressing the person, separate the person from the behaviour that you want to focus attention on.

This in no way means that you absolve the person of the responsibility for the consequences of his/her actions. If there are errors, they need to be pointed out, corrected *and* worked upon. But not by attacking the very being of the person with harsh words.

By taking the wind away, the balloon cannot be expected to fly.

If the person feels that he or she is, himself or herself, a mistake, dumb, stupid, a loser or beyond redemption, then how will he/she work on the issue? The idea is to get the person to see his/her action objectively, take responsibility for it, and look for ways of addressing, reducing and preventing errors.

So how do we do this?

1. Separate the behaviour from the person

Instead of calling Feroze dumb and stupid one can say, "Feroze, you work out such complicated beats in music to keep time. Think of maths like musical beats. We will look up some maths exercises linked to music for you to practise. Now go over your answer script carefully, *check for mistakes and try not to repeat them.*"

If a child throws something and it breaks, instead of calling him 'destructive', say, "That was a wrong thing to do. You have broken the toy and now we cannot fix it." Focus on the behaviour and show him the consequences of his action.

Instead of calling the child 'unkind', 'cruel' or 'mean', we could say, "that was not a nice thing to do" or "that is an unkind thing to say" or "that is a mean thing to do" and add "and we don't want to be unkind and make the person feel sad, right?"

Rather than calling the employee a loser, one could say, "This is a surprising error coming from you since you have performed well in similar situations earlier. Go back to the skills you learnt during your training and analyse where you slipped up. You will have your answer."

Instead of demolishing the person and his or her self esteem with harsh words, we try and centre in on the problem, talk about that and if possible, help with suggestions on how to deal with it.

There could however be situations that are extreme, with behaviour totally unacceptable, that need firm action. But these are not the norm. Here we are talking about the more common actions and interactions.

2. Practising Externalisation

There are also situations when a person seeks help regarding a personal problem/behaviour trait causing issues for him/her internally and also in dealings with the external world. Practising externalisation is one method of helping the person.

The concept of externalisation in Narrative Therapy is interesting. *This* needs to be done under professional guidance. *What* needs to be externalised and how, requires careful supervision.

Once again, this technique is not to diminish the person's taking accountability for his actions. Rather, through externalisation, the attempt is to address the problem and prevent the unhelpful effects of the problem on him and those around.

Through this technique, people are helped to create a distance and separate themselves from the problem.

"The person is not the problem; the problem is the problem." These are the words of Michael White, one of the developers of Narrative therapy.

The counsellor guides the client to personify or objectify the problem being discussed. For example, if a person believes that he is an angry person and his angry outbursts create issues, he might see anger as residing within him; as if he and anger are one. He personalises the problem and identifies with it. For example, he could say, *"I am an angry person."*

Through externalisation and by asking appropriate questions, anger is seen as something outside of oneself. This gives one a feeling of control over the problem that is making one behave in a way that one does not like.

Naming the problem in the person's own words, describes the person's own experience of the problem. For example, instead of anger, the person could call it 'jaws', 'monster' or 'scowl' or simply 'it' or 'the'. He could even give it an image.

There is then something more concrete to handle, instead of it being just a generic term. He can gradually build more trust in himself and not feel defined by the problem and in turn it makes him feel more empowered to deal with it.

How do these processes help?

There is often a feeling of relief that there is more to the person than the overarching problem. It supports the person to see a way out of a negative thought loop and replace it with positive thoughts; and move towards a 'preferred story'. Talking about the alternative stories in his life will make him feel better about himself and his life.

The deeper understanding can help the person reclaim his/her life from the hold of the problem. In the course of the conversation the person's own resources for dealing with the problem and otherwise too, are also revealed. So the internal strengths also come to the fore.

Both these techniques—of separating the person from the behaviour when correcting somebody; and helping the person see the problem as outside of himself/herself instead of it being a part of him/her, through the externalisation process, have one thing in common.

They both see the individual as much more than just the problem; with the capacity to harness the resources, strengths and skills within the person to deal with the situation.

The next time anger and harsh words want to get the better of us here is a line to think about:

> ***"Raise your words, not your voice. It is the rain that grows flowers, not thunder."***
>
> **—Rumi**

Introspection

1. Do you remember hurtful, harsh words spoken to you that have stayed with you? What has been their impact on you?
2. How would you respond and protect yourself when someone lashes out at you using foul language and demeaning words?

3. Has there been a time when you wanted to say something really nasty out of anger or frustration but controlled yourself? What helped you do this?
4. After reading the chapter on harsh words what technique would you like to remember to practise before saying something harsh?
5. Think of hurtful language that you may have used. What was your intention behind the communication? Did you achieve the result and was it beneficial in the long run?

Given a chance to reword unkind language that you may have used, how would you rephrase your sentence? Keep in mind the importance of separating the person from the act. The idea is not to punish the person and make the person feel small and bad, but to help solve the problem, as is said in the technique of positive discipline.

21

No Place Like Home

But What's Your Definition of Home?

'Mid pleasures and palaces though we may roam

Be it ever so humble there's no place like home...' (Lyrics of a song by John Howard Payne)

Recently, I met a friend after a long time and I asked her, "So where are you living now?" Without a moment's hesitation she said, "In my head."

This sounded unusual, so I asked, "And what does that mean?"

Her instantaneous response was, "Exactly what I said. I have two permanent addresses; my email id and my mind. I live in them and carry them with me wherever I go. I can be contacted on one and I physically live in the other at all times."

"If you're referring to a house of brick and mortar, then that changes all the time, depending on where my work takes me; and where I choose to go. I have lived in more than fifty apartments across the globe and at innumerable hotels."

I told her I would feel pretty disoriented waking up in brand new surroundings ever so often. I needed stability and continuity, which also meant continuity in my living space and at least some continuity in the people around me.

Her answer was clear, "I find attachment to a geographical location and a house very restrictive. My mind has no boundaries. It gives me the happy combination of stability and freedom."

Differing definitions of Home

This conversation got me thinking.

I could not see myself living her life. But I could appreciate that she, unlike me and many others, did not have the need to go home to her bed and couch. She was a home for herself; and the external trappings of concrete dimensions made no difference to her.

Freedom and independence, unburdened by mundane chores of running a home, works well for some. Yet, it is also true that there are those who live alone and need to travel, but do not make this choice of living within themselves. At some point they want to go back home.

We hear of people who spend their 'working' years far away from the place where they were brought up; but after retirement want to go back 'home' to their comfort zone.

A gentleman in his sixties, having lived abroad for years, urged his parents not to update their furniture. In his core, he wanted the security of his childhood home to remain undisturbed in a highly volatile world.

And then there are homes where people have lived over generations. Their very identity is interwoven with the bricks. There is a sense of pride, history, legacy all of which goes into making them the individuals they are.

So what does home mean to people?

I spoke to people of different ages and here are the responses:

> *"Family, sense of belonging, refuge, comfort, memories." "Where I can relax, be myself and feel safe, feel loved and cared for." "Where I have someone to talk to and share my feelings with." "Where I get a feeling of stability in an otherwise very unpredictable world." "The aroma and taste of home food, trust, relief." "A place with a breathing, living presence that I can call my own."*

It boils down to what resonates with us.

Homes have significant memories attached to them and the heart wants to revisit and relive those moments. I have seen people go back to a place they once lived in and display a totally new dimension of themselves.

A middle-aged lady visited her childhood home. The tactile touch of the rooms and walls that stored her memories helped her reconnect with a lost aspect of herself and she broke into a happy song she had sung as a child. Her difficult years of marriage had stolen her cheer.

Another gentleman took his son and grandchild to visit the 'family home' in another country. He had childhood memories of their home before the partition of India. He was fortunate to find the house still there and the new owners graciously allowed them to spend time there as the gentleman took pictures and narrated incidents that he remembered.

Houses change owners; but a home lives inside you

It is a feeling, a concept, which you manifest into the place where you physically stay. During the pandemic when travel was restricted, work and education from home was the new normal and socialising not being possible, 'home' was where we were most of the time.

How do we create a happy space for ourselves and our family?

There is no magic formula, but some basic thoughts can be shared.

1. Create an ambience of peace

A six-year-old boy was being mischievous and his teacher said she would inform his parents. "No, no. Don't call them. I am tensioning!" was the child's response. At that tender age he used the word appropriately; meaning he could actually feel the pressure he experienced in his own home.

There is enough stress and judging outside the home. Don't add to it in your personal space.

We can begin with ourselves. Just be conscious of the shared space. And remember the cardinal rule: 'Do unto others as you would have them do unto you.'

2. Set some basic rules for the house

Meals to be had together, no watching the mobile or television at that time; clear up your dishes from the table; don't litter the common use areas, including living room and toilets; try and keep your room tidy; mind the volume while listening to any device. If followed, these rules help set standards and reduce scope for everyday friction.

Have fun together in the common free time by playing games like carrom, ludo or cards. A family used the dining table as a makeshift table tennis table. Another sent signature video greetings for special occasions with impromptu family concerts which they recorded in their home space. These created warm abiding memories.

3. Homes have unique aromas

Make food interesting, not necessarily elaborate. Serve favourite dishes in rotation. Involvement of different members breaks the monotony in jobs such as cooking or laying out the table beautifully. A young man happily reminisced, *"I remember laying out the table for our Christmas dinner, bringing out the beautiful bone china crockery, wine gasses, silver candle holders. Everyone enjoyed it and it made me feel special too."*

Specific essential oils, incense, after shaves, perfumes are also associated with home. A gentleman who has been an NRI for three decades uses only sandalwood soap. It's his memory of home.

Creating a 'perfect' home can be exhausting, mentally and physically. Overlooking a little dust or a room not absolutely spic and span, is well worth it.

A friend once said to me, *"I feel a home is a place to celebrate and enjoy the warmth of life, togetherness, sharing and caring. We can have an old and shabby sofa set but that cannot stop us from inviting friends over and having a great time over just tea, toast and jam or tea and samosas. It is the vibes of the home that are so important. Welcoming, open and warm."*

4. Multiple definitions of home

The beauty is that each one of us can add something, to how we would like our home to be. It is so personal. You can create it your way, within the walls. But we need to ensure that it does not become an imposition on the others who share it with us. It is everyone's home.

A middle-aged person reminisced about how the summer holiday visits to his grandmother's house were always tension ridden. *"I can understand the need for discipline but carried too far it is counterproductive like everything that is done in excess. She had a fetish for keeping the bedcover totally stretched and tightly drawn. I was scared to sleep on it because each time I got off the bed it had to be got back to its pristine condition. I could not eat anywhere other than the dining table, even if it was just fruits like a banana."*

And to finish, I am tempted to go back to where I started, with my friend's view of living 'in her head'. Having a home of brick and stone and being free are not really contradictory.

Kahlil Gibran explains this so beautifully:

For that which is boundless in you
Abides in the mansion of the sky,
Whose door is the morning mist, and
Whose windows are the songs and the
silences of night.

We are free in spirit. That is our privilege.

Yet, most of us also need brick and mortar to house our physical bodies; where we live together with our loved ones, keep our belongings, create memories, have an address to come back to; and, if the need arises, move on to another address, with the spirit in us as free as ever.

> ***"The magic thing about home is that it feels good to leave, and it feels even better to come back."***
>
> **—Wendy Wunder**

Introspection

1. Do you have a 'me' place in your home that you can retreat to? What does it mean to you?
2. In today's world when interior designers are often the ones who design our homes, how would you make a home distinctly yours'?
3. Think of homes you like to visit or have memories of visiting as a child. What drew you to them? Do people feel attracted to visiting your home?

22

Roles We Fulfil in Personal & Professional Lives

Managing with Awareness

When I hear my two-year-old granddaughter talk, it is fascinating to notice how easily she refers to herself in the third person; and even more interesting is, how comfortably we reply in the third person to her, while referring to ourselves.

She takes her name; and we name ourselves according to what she calls us. This is a very common phenomenon. The child does it unconsciously and adults do it consciously, just to make the communication easier.

I realised when we verbally call ourselves by the 'role' name like 'Dadi' or 'Dadu', the significance of that role becomes far more 'real'. It is like a reminder. I found myself thinking of my grandmother's role in my life.

Her smell, touch and blind faith in me, which even today acts like a yardstick of not doing anything that would make her sad. Her words of reassurance, when something went wrong; the comforting sight of her sitting in the easy chair waiting for us, when she knew we would be visiting; her putting a yogurt dot on my head and chanting a mantra before I went for an exam, which boosted my confidence a hundredfold...all came back to mind.

I wonder what memories I would leave with my granddaughter. That is something only time will tell. But the start of all this introspection and reminiscing was to do with the act of calling oneself by a certain name. It led to a chain reaction of associated thoughts and feelings.

Nurturing the 'being you' role

We all have a name or names that we respond to, when addressed. The stimulus for that response comes from the other person. When the stimulus is generated internally, it can be a very useful tool; as I discovered not very long ago. Let me explain this.

I have a fear of closed spaces and was stuck in an elevator. Panic set in. Then I remembered the words of an uncle, "When alone and feeling defeated by something, just chide yourself sharply, telling yourself to get your act together. You are your own best friend."

I did just that. As an observer I peered through the inky blackness, looked at my crumpled figure in the corner and said, "Sumita, get yourself together. Breathe deeply. Soon someone will need to use the elevator and will know there is no electricity. And you will get help."

It helped. Loudly calling out my name as if I was someone else, talking to Sumita, made me listen to logic even in the midst of a noisy pounding heart. Slowly I got a hold over myself and waited.

This example is not to talk about how one should deal with panic attacks. That requires professional guidance. It is simply to highlight how, consciously taking on the role of being my own friend, helped me handle the situation.

Roles carry the weight of expectations

Role is the name of our relationship vis-a-vis ourselves, another person or being. Each one of us relates to those around us from various aspects of ourselves. These roles have specific names—mother, father, child, brother, sister, leader, teacher, doctor, friend...the list goes on. Each role carries the weight of certain expectations, from others and from ourselves. Even if a role is thrust on us, we do have a choice about our attitude to it; and not make it more difficult for ourselves.

Through life we are navigating roles and their inherent responsibilities on the personal and professional front. But underneath them all is 'you'. Other than the interpersonal intelligence, what is of prime importance is intra-personal awareness; self care, resolving internal conflicts, building self esteem and self respect. In other words the 'self role' has to be well nurtured to build a strong base.

The more comfortable we are with ourselves, without the fear of rejection or constantly looking for validation, the more in tune we will be with our core self/belief/values and less likely to be at conflict with ourselves. There will be a consistency in our behaviour and a confidence in our actions.

Awareness of what we are seeking from others in terms of affirmation or recognition is important, so that we don't fall into a trap of continuously looking for it; and to please others, move away from our true self in our actions.

Scope of each role—avoid conditioning

Famous lines by William Shakespeare:

> *All the world's a stage, and all men and women merely players;*
>
> *They have their exits and their entrances, and one man in his time plays many parts...*

There are times when we need to consciously remind ourselves of the scope of a specific role, because the default mode would be to simply slip into what we have been conditioned to do.

A gentleman candidly told me, "*My son and I had got into some sort of an ego fight. It was an argument that I was treating like a war, which I was determined to win at any cost. I had got conditioned to it. A well wisher later reminded me that I was the father and my responsibility went far beyond just winning. I could win the argument but lose much more. That was a timely eye opener and my perspective changed.*"

Crafting a role

Making a note of our significant roles helps prioritise them and enhances the quality of the delivery of responsibilities. Here are some tips on what we could do to handle roles better.

1. Spreading ourselves too thin, over innumerable roles, detracts from our effectiveness

We have time constrictions and the demand on our time can make it difficult to deliver on all fronts. Prioritising what we consider are our important roles, helps in better time and quality management. Having a disciplined schedule also helps. Many children living far away from their parents call once a week on a specific day. Meeting a group of old friends once a month, giving time to an NGO on a regular basis could be commitments we make to fulfil certain roles over and above the regular roles we have in our homes and workplace.

We may reject certain roles because they clash with our values. Example: being a partner in a firm that does not have clean dealings.

2. *Some role requirements can be unpleasant, but need to be done*

One could have the role in a company to manage cost cutting and this could require laying off people. It is a difficult and painful job.

Verbalising the role that we are playing often gives a meaning to the task and our attitude might change.

3. *Some roles change with time*

Flexibility is needed in fulfilling the role as the scope changes. A parent, for example, needs to step back and yet be available. Children become caregivers to ageing parents. Parents, with advancing age might turn to children for advice.

4. *Each role requires different qualities and skills*

Some may come naturally and some, we need to train ourselves into. You may have reservations about a career choice made by a child, but the parent role demands that you support your child's dreams, while informing him/her about the challenges.

The skill is in how we communicate our support and belief in the child; and also help him/her do a reality check. Teaching the child to make an informed decision in life is the responsibility of the parent.

5. Delivering role expectations can be challenging emotionally as well

Balancing different roles through societal pressures, personal stressors, expectations and reality is an art. There are times when there is confusion about what we should do.

However simplistic it may sound, one way to help ourselves could be, to mentally take a moment, when we just call ourselves by the name of the role we are fulfilling and act accordingly. It helps with a purpose and a structure. In all of these we need to be true to our basic values.

6. Sometimes, taking inspiration from a role model that we may have of a person in that role, gives direction

When in confusion we could also put ourselves in the shoes of the other person. For example, a person needs support and we don't know how to help. I could ask myself, "How would I have liked my friend to respond, if I was in the same situation?" Sometimes it helps to get feedback about ourselves or asking the person what he or she would like us to do to deliver the responsibility of the role better.

7. Role boundaries are important

Accepting what is possible to do and what is not; and learning to say 'no'. Fulfilling all roles to perfection is often unrealistic. Accepting our own challenges, knowing ourselves and staying close to who we are, helps in limiting the stress of expectations from others.

8. *It is a good idea to objectively re-evaluate our 'performance' in important roles to 'grow' in them*

Professionally and personally—how well am I doing and what are my expectations from myself? For this we need to set specific goals.

As a teacher I might need to learn how to make the classes more interactive online and offline. As a manager I might want to step up the quality of my presentations. Personally, I might want to learn the tools of mindfulness. As a parent I might want to learn to be more patient. As a partner I might need to be more present. As a friend I need to be more mindful of keeping in touch and wishing on birthdays and anniversaries.

It helps in creating a balance so that our roles on the personal and professional fronts are looked after. It requires planning, discipline and consistency.

How do you know that you are doing justice to your role?

Be the person, whose presence is valued and cherished and absence is noticed, whatever role you are in.

> *"We play many roles in our life, but do we play each role intelligently and with a sense of responsibility? This is what we really need to ask ourselves."*
>
> —**Sri Sri Ravi Shankar**

Introspection

1. What are the significant roles you play in your life? How would you prioritise them?
2. Think of a role you play that you give more attention to, so that you can grow in it with depth and understanding?
3. Of the roles you play, is there any that you find overly stressful and demanding? Can you do something to help yourself?
4. Which is the role you fit into most easily? Can you explain why this is so?
5. Managing the various roles we play requires skilful balancing. Sometimes we over commit ourselves. Time is limited and so are resources. Check and see if you are comfortable with your commitments so that you can do justice to them.

23

Good Morning Messages

How to Make them More Meaningful

I have woken up to multiple 'good morning' messages. Many are quotations in various fonts:

- Of blessings, prayers and tips, on how to lead a better life;
- Quotes placed on backgrounds of pretty images, paintings, nature's beauty from across the world;
- Video clips of 'wellness' gurus giving a capsule dose on the secrets of leading a better life;
- Excerpts of songs—either with just the audio or with images, on various nuances of life.

I browsed through them with mixed feelings; happy that I had these people in my social circle. The individual messages especially made me feel warmer, because they had a personal thought behind pressing the 'send' arrow.

At the same time I did not invest much attention on them. With a cursory glance they were deleted. The communication seemed incomplete, not really leaving any dent.

Many of the group forwards were repetitions from other groups or individuals and I deleted them almost on default mode; not worth wasting time on; and also because they clogged up the phone.

Blindly pressing the 'forward' arrow means one is not thinking of the receiver.

Why do we send these messages?

Habit, 'time-pass', genuine desire to reach out, to feel a sense of belonging and connection, the need to share something that we find meaningful or beautiful—it could be some or all of these or even other drivers.

What kind of messages actually caught my deeper attention?

I realised there were a couple that were sent on a group which were impactful.

One had the individual taking personal pictures of a feature from her garden and writing a catchy caption with it. Her posts elicited multiple responses from the group members. There was engagement; a gap day from her end was noticed and missed.

More interestingly, the posts led to further conversations. For example, a picture of a fresh crop of lemon, mangoes or even an unusual flower led to exchanges of sharing of recipes using the vegetable or fruit; comments with personal nostalgia were triggered by the image; discussions on the details of the flower; or the sharing of some other picture taken by a group member, who felt enthused.

It generated curiosity, bonhomie and genuine connection.

Another individual sent videos and messages that highlighted gentler, softer and happier events which are often neglected in the face of all the negativity—a healing balm of hope in the troubled world around us. These were uplifting and set the mood for the day.

What makes a 'Good Morning' message interactive?

What I gathered was that there was a healthy dose of the person in the message that generated conversation.

Instead of an impersonal 'forward', the person had taken time and trouble framing it and had enjoyed the process.

Over time an individual may develop a kind of 'niche' message style that we associate with the person, which makes the message unique and personalised. That however does not mean cramping the person to sending only one kind of message.

At the start of a day we respond better to messages that spell hope, cheer and are relatable.

How can we get the elusive personal stamp on messages that we may be in the habit of sharing?

1. A little home work

Give some thought to why we want to send the message first thing in the morning. It is the start of a new day.

- What impact will the message have?
- Would I like to receive the same message?
- What do I do with the stereotypical impersonal images and words that are sent to me?
- When I see certain names of the senders, do I automatically and mechanically press the delete button without giving the post a second glance?

Why do I do this? How can I ensure that receivers of my posts do not do the same?

2. Who am I sending the message to?

For example, for some people who have very limited opportunity to step out of their homes, connection with people through phones is essential.

It is possible that the good morning message means that they are remembered and has a lot of emotional importance. Suddenly stopping it might lead to causing hurt.

In such cases, along with the messages, it would be even more relevant if I make the effort of calling on some days to wish the person.

3. Is my message suited to the audience?

People go through all kinds of experiences. I need to be sensitive to this so that the message does not appear to be cheeky or inappropriate. For example, a message that sounds like I 'know it all'; or messages about going for healthy walks, to a person who is bedridden.

4. To make my posts 'mine' I need to put a bit of me into it.

It is a greeting from 'me' to 'you'. Creative, meaningful and worthwhile for the receiver and me to spend time on. It also shows respect for the viewer.

I need to know what is important to me, what I feel deeply about and what I want to share with others.

5. A short message and not a preachy one.

It must be genuine. Hollow and shallow words are easy to see through. I do not need to send a message everyday like a compulsion.

If I have the time, the content and the desire, I could send posts suited to the group or the individual; and space the days, so that it is not a burden for me; and I do not get repetitive. It also allows me the opportunity to explore different aspects of myself.

For example, there is a lot of emphasis on the need for gratitude to better our mental health.

What if I use a little bit of time on some mornings to think of something that I am grateful for and post that as my wake up message?

It serves a dual purpose. Experiencing gratitude is a deeply rewarding emotion for me. Expressing and sharing it makes it a richer feel for me; and, it is possible that a receiver too relates to it.

Perhaps, I could get more adventurous on some days and add appropriate visuals with some of my lines.

Someone I know takes exquisite pictures of the sky in different seasons, at various times of the day, capturing multiple moods and gives a caption with it. And the lines are a reflection on life too.

Yet another captures images of funny, touching, interesting sights on the street and posts them with suitable lines as 'thought for the day'.

The bottom line is that the message should be sincere. Ideally, at the start of a day, it is nice to receive a positive message.

> ***"My happiness is infectious and will get passed on through my posts."***
>
> **—Anonymous**

Introspection

1. Are there good morning messages that you receive that resonate with you? What is special about them?
2. Going beyond just good morning messages, what care do you take before forwarding videos and posts that you receive?
3. If you enjoy wishing friends good morning through messages, how would you customise it such that it has **you** in it?

24

Senior Years

Planning for the Journey Ahead; Reflections of a Senior Citizen

For a senior citizen, flipping through the pages of a photo album can evoke mixed responses. Nostalgia, yes with rekindled memories that bring a smile and a warm flush to the heart.

There could also be a feeling of loss—of youth, of people in the album who are no more; a desire to rewind the clock and do a few things differently...

But...not possible. We know age creeps up on us. The pictures are evidence. Life is finite.

So what can we do?

We could plan for our senior years to the extent possible. For those very senior, or ailing, we could assist them in having a respectful and dignified farewell and help them know that they lived a meaningful life.

A letter to the age called Senior Years:

Dear Senior Years,

I know I am getting there. In so many little ways, you announce your presence.

- I forget the name of the movie I watched last week.

- If something rolls under the bed, I holler for assistance to retrieve it.
- Walking up or down stairs or slopes, I mutter if there is no banister to clutch on to.
- I sit ravenously hungry at the dining table and then manage to plough through only a quarter of the delectable stroganoff before giving up.
- Listening to bygone days' bygone music, the morning somehow slips into late afternoon, without my even being aware of it.
- Playing with grandchildren I feel terribly challenged, when having to navigate technology.

You get the picture, right?!

Of course you do! You orchestrated it.

But… Let's play a game shall we?

Now that I am somewhat aware of your game plan, dear senior years, I need to chalk out my moves so that we have a healthy match, without you vanquishing me from point go. I realise that checkmate will be your call; but you know what—I've restructured my strategy—we will get there, hand in hand, as friends.

So what do I do?

You keep moving up, while I do what I need to

I understand that you cannot really alter your path but I have the ability to exercise choices and make that path a less bumpy, slippery, steep, downward spiral. And though I may have been a little slow in comprehending this, I can try and do so now.

To start with, I will not fight you; but accept that you are nature's companion to me, not my enemy.

Next, I will try and strengthen those areas where your intimacy can make me anxious and wobbly. After all you don't want an uninteresting, uninspired partner on your journey, do you?

So I will keep myself attractive, physically and mentally. I have been told by innumerable mentors that a judicious diet, physical exercise and mental recharge is the secret to this.

Easier said than done. But my desire to keep pace with you as your charming mate will keep me disciplined. I don't want you to consume me out of sheer irritation!

I want the journey to be one where we can share camaraderie, empathy, kindness towards each other; and also allow time to nurture human connections, hobbies, travelling and doing nothing too.

I would like to continue having a purpose to my day so that I wake up with energy and hope.

My responsibilities in this senior years journey

You know senior years, along with enjoying my journey with you, there are certain responsibilities that I need to complete. For my own self.

- If it is useful later for those after me, even better. I need to record my family history and stories of individuals in my family, which I have found fascinating. I could collect stories from those older than me in the family and add what I have heard so that these are not lost forever. There are times when I wish I had someone I could go to, to verify a detail.

- And if along the way you decide to give me a jolt for some reason, I would like to have the resilience, strength and grace to accept it. For doing this I need the blessings of gratitude and the love of those I care for. I would like to also, consciously, be a source of strength and comfort to them and contribute in whatever way I can.
- I realise that I get tired nowadays of managing things; and for that matter, also dealing with heavy emotional baggage. They make me drag my already weary feet. So I have decided to shed weight. Of course the physical kind is a great idea but also the other kind. 'Winding down' is the term used so that life is more manageable and less overwhelming, just dealing with daily maintenance.
- Clearing out cupboards of unused clothes, giving away curios and extra crockery, even giving money to those I want to. It gives a lot of happiness.
- Perhaps even moving into a smaller place, if necessary. And if need be, and at the cost of touching on a sensitive topic, be open to investing in a suitable retirement home, which requires a lot of planning and scouting around for.
- The more difficult part is the emotional negativity which takes longer, more sustained effort but is possible to cast off. And that brings a lot of personal relief. Harbouring grudges, regret, anger, guilt can be draining.
- What also brings joy is to connect to people I have been meaning to but never got around to making that call or that visit. I would like to do that and tell those close to me what I feel for them and their

place in my life. I know that I cherish words of love said to me but I have been remiss in doing the same. Sometimes feelings, however 'understood' need to be spelt out.

Planning mundane essentials

Planning for senior years also entails the more mundane but essential aspects like:

- Health and life insurance, planning a realistic retirement budget, keeping in mind the rising cost of living; learning important skills like online banking, keeping bank accounts and lockers with nominees, managing finances judiciously and if necessary with the help of a trusted expert; signing up with an organisation that provides care to elders (a large section of us live in nuclear families and need to look after ourselves).
- Since I am totally unaware about when you will decide to declare checkmate, I would like to try and leave a peaceful legacy for my family. It will give me a sense of calm too.
- Making a will, informing my family about the whereabouts of important documents and keys, keeping my financial and other papers updated, neatly filed and without encumbrances, are a few of the things I can do. It helps me too, you know. I don't want them to remember me with angst about having placed them in a cauldron of complications.
- And finally, my friend senior years, I know I cannot plan for all exigencies or control all aspects but to the extent possible and 'plannable', I will do my

best, so that we are happy together and as stress-less as feasible.

- With this 'awakening' that I have recently had, I am now also getting more conscious about how those who are very senior feel, when their opinion is not taken in decisions regarding their own lives, when possible.
- We all like to feel that we have some control over our own lives, regardless of our age. It gives us a feeling of self respect and dignity—I count or what I say or feel matters. I have contributed meaningfully in my time and would enjoy continuing to do so. Of course, there are situations when an emergency or a chronic problem like dementia or Alzheimer's makes it difficult.

I'm happy we had this time together—you and I—to help me sort out my own thoughts regarding you, Senior Years.

Cheers to our future together!

> *"Age is an issue of mind over matter. If you don't mind, it doesn't matter."*
>
> **—Mark Twain**

Introspection

1. Do you agree that one needs to plan for one's senior years when reasonably young? Have you thought about your senior years?
2. Think of a senior person you know or someone close to you. How could you make life a little more meaningful for the person?

3. Can you think of all the activities possible in senior years that would add value to your life?
4. Ageing happens to every living creature on earth. How would you make the process and the experience of senior years more pleasant for yourself?

25

Being Me

Is My Persona just a Social Construct? Or is there More to It?

"I am trying to figure out how much of me is a response to what others feel about me and how much is really me." This is from a thirty-two year old who is on a mission of self discovery.

Is being 'me' just a social construct?

I thought about his statement and said to myself, "The whole is me but is most of me just a 'social construct'?"

Do we live much of our lives merely responding to others? Such as:

- Trying to please people; bothering about what people will think about our action and so trying to behave such that we fit in.
- Doing things as a mode of defiance and perhaps regretting it later; doing things because others are doing it and not stepping out of the surge to see if our actions really resonate with us.
- Taking things up because someone challenges us and not because we really wish to or believe in the issue.

- Behaving in a way that is expected of us in the particular gathering or by a particular person; seeking validation and feeling confident only if we get the nod of approval.
- Being a different 'me' depending on who we are with and sometimes getting confused about which 'me' we are most comfortable with—the 'inspirer' leading from the front and making all the major decisions at certain times.
- Or, being the quiet, lost in the crowd follower at other times?

***"We are all creatures conditioned by the environment and the 'socialisation process'. This has been our journey through our evolution from uni-cellular organisms to complex beings,"* remarked a friend.**

'Me' also needs to belong

Many of us have heard the song, 'No man is an island, no man lives alone...' (the poem is by John Donne). We all want to **belong.** We want to feel connected.

We want to belong to a person, a family, a group, in our workplace, amongst our friends... We also have a need to be needed.

We would like our absence to be missed, our words to count, our presence to be valued. We want to love and be loved.

We want to have that 'specialness' about us. But we don't want to be an outcast either.

So, we want to be 'me' and we also want that 'me' to gel and belong. And in that process, the defining line between 'me' and society often gets blurred.

We also want to own our uniqueness and this sometimes leads us to resisting all of the above.

This is not a weakness if we can find the balance between integrating and not losing our individuality.

The inner me

There is a lot of talk today about getting in touch with the inner you—finding some quiet time searching for your core in the tsunami of living life. It is like having a date with yourself.

When we are interested in someone, we are curious about the person and ask questions: What makes you truly happy? What are the things that bother you? Are there things you would like to change about yourself? How would you like to be remembered?

The questions are many and we can customise them to what matters to us.

In this case we are curious about ourselves and have a self conversation. It helps in understanding ourselves, questioning ourselves and in the process getting a more defined picture of 'me'.

Closely linked with this is the Japanese concept of Ikigai—'Me' getting up and close with our individual meaning for living. And that is an intimate introduction to being me.

This reminds me of the activities for children which I enjoy doing—Finding Waldo or Where's Wally—in pages of books where he is apparently lost somewhere in the blur of activities that are illustrated. It is an effort and requires focus and concentration but sooner or later Waldo or Wally can be located—in the crowd but distinct.

Is there a distinctiveness about me?

'Me' is evolving, growing and changing

I don't believe there is the right or correct answer, a *'lock kiya jaye'* type me. Maybe deep, deep inside there is a flame burning steadily that does not waver, but in many other aspects —views, attitudes, beliefs—the 'me' is not constant.

It is evolving, growing and changing—an ongoing process. It is to do with our personal life experiences; how we respond to them, what choices we make and what we take away from them.

Sometimes we go happily with the flow of things happening around. At other times we step out and take the scenic route or the short cut; and sometimes, we simply succumb to the pressure.

So if someone we have met after a long time is surprised by a certain response from us and says, *"Oh this is not you. What happened?"* our reply could be, *"This is me but the 'now' me. Since we last met and today, 'life' has happened."*

And this was possible because we were flexible and open to changes and hopefully used our wisdom while adapting.

The 'me' that is not sustainable is the one that follows someone blindly and tries to become that person. We cannot live someone else's life and become a copy.

Understanding and accepting what we value about being 'me'

Education, challenges, exposure to hugely contrasting climes in every sense of the word, get us to question ourselves.

We go through a lot of churning—not being able to let go of the 'me' we knew and were comfortable with; and the reworked me taking shape inside us.

Sometimes, in fact more often than not, both co-exist.

A person got on to an aeroplane to go overseas and there was a visible change in his being.

On being told this, his response was, "I can feel myself feeling freer. Like a cloak being taken off. I am one aspect of myself here in my hometown and it is my default mode. I am not even conscious of it. But whenever I travel abroad another aspect of me emerges. I play hide and seek with myself—depending on where I am."

"But who are you more at ease with?" he was asked.

Thinking a while he replied, "I feel more like me when I feel free and that makes me happy." He had understood and accepted what he valued. How he would walk the future was a decision he would have to make.

Not directly related to this but an interesting insight comes to us from a well-known legend. It is a story about life told to a grandson by his grandfather using the example of two wolves that reside inside us and there is a battle between them. He talked about one wolf that has jealousy, anger, greed, arrogance, resentment, self pity, guilt, false pride, and lies. The other wolf has joy, peace, kindness, generosity, empathy, serenity, humility, love, hope, compassion and faith. The curious grandson thought about it and asked, "Grandfather, which wolf wins?" Grandfather replied, "The one you feed."

The choice is with us. As Viktor E. Frankl is known to have said in his book *Man's Search for Meaning*, "Everything can be taken from a man but one thing: the last of the human freedoms—to choose one's attitude in any given set of circumstances, to choose one's own way."

The Psychological make-up

So yes we are all complex social constructs—we live in a society, in certain cultures and we are defined by them to a very large extent.

We are also moulded by our childhood experiences. Yet, the same scenario can have two entities who have grown up in the same set up, responding entirely differently to a situation because of that elusive 'me' factor.

The psychological makeup of the individual is different. And that is also where being ME happens. It is possible that in the course of events there will be two conflicting 'Me-s' inside us engaged in a duel—with contradictory views, beliefs, stands.

We need to resolve this internally and with time we will come to accept the 'me' we are more comfortable and confident with and stay with that one.

At the metaphysical level

This conversation can be taken to the level of the metaphysical where it is said that there is nothing like you and me—this 'you', 'I' or 'me' is all a part of one energy, one Universal Consciousness. We are mere specks in this vast cosmic canvas and we all dissolve into this one life force.

On the other hand, we are living, breathing human beings who have been blessed with the opportunity of existing on this planet for a certain number of years, however insignificant it may be relative to cosmic time.

This lifespan is what we have as an individual and it is important to us. And with this opportunity comes the responsibility of navigating our own little fragile vehicle, with concern and care; so that it can add a wee bit of enrichment to the dynamic one energy when it once again dissolves into it.

So one could say to the young man on the mission of self discovery:

There is only one you and you are your responsibility. Live it, love it, protect it, nurture it, cherish it and celebrate it.

> ***"You have to learn to trust yourself. You are the only one who knows who you truly are and how it really is for you."***
>
> **—Joe Duncan**

Introspection

1. Looking back at your life, which are the areas in which you have changed considerably—in your views, behaviour, habits, attitude? Are you comfortable with it? Do you feel you have grown as a person?

2. If asked what your Ikigai is, your personal meaning for life and what makes you interested in a new day, what answer would you give? How has it evolved over time?

About the Author

Sumita Banerjea is an author, educator and counsellor. An alumna of the Convent of Jesus and Mary, and St. Stephen's College, New Delhi, she has done her PhD in History on 'Crime Against Women And By Women In Bengal In The 18th And 19th Centuries' from Jamia Millia Islamia.

She has written school textbooks on Geography and English and has also written for various newspapers and magazines.

Sumita conceptualised and edited a series of English books for students of Middle School written by Senior School students. These were collections of stories and poems, each of which was also illustrated by students. Entitled *Voices of Today*, these books were used by multiple schools across the country and were covered widely by newspapers and television channels.

Two short story collections authored by her, *Chowringhee Charms* (Readomania 2021) and *Playhouse Park Street* (Readomania 2023) received wonderful reviews.

She is trained in psychological counselling, conducts workshops for corporates, teachers and students, and occasionally writes a blog on personal development.

Sumita loves to experience life in a myriad different ways: travelling, teaching, writing, counselling, listening to happenings in the lives of people from various walks of life, and telling stories. She lives in Kolkata.

Readomania exists to nurture, curate, and bring to you content you love. We are a publishing house that takes pride in encouraging talent, new or old, and provide a wonderful platform for awesome stories.

We make this possible in multiple ways.

The first as an independent publishing house. Readomania boasts of multiple imprints across various categories—fiction, nonfiction, children, to name a few. An eclectic mix of content for its readers, when you read a Readomania title, you enter a world that's yours, supported by unique and quality narratives.

The second, as an online publishing platform for writers—a place to share stories, poems, opinions, travelogues, a way to explore your creative talent. Available as premium, as well as free-to-read content across multiple genres, the reader is spoilt for choice.

Join us in this journey, as we explore, develop, and present stories to our readers and audiences. Welcome to the world of Readomania, get ready to craft stories that enrich lives.

You can visit us at: www.readomania.com

www.ingramcontent.com/pod-product-compliance
Lightning Source LLC
LaVergne TN
LVHW091314150826
845673LV00006B/1639

* 9 7 8 9 3 9 1 8 0 0 7 8 9 *